PENGUIN BOOKS

Un Amico Italiano

Luca Spaghetti was born in Rome, and his surname really is Spaghetti. Meeting American writer Elizabeth Gilbert in September of 2003 changed his life: Luca became one of the best-loved characters in Gilbert's international bestseller *Eat, Pray, Love*, and to this day he receives letters from readers asking him if he really exists. Luca lives in Rome; he loves Roman food and American music. This is his first book. Visit him at www.LucaSpaghetti.com.

Antony Shugaar is a translator and journalist with a special interest in Mediterranean Europe. He received a 2007 NEA fellowship for his translation of *Sandokan* by Nanni Balestrini, and has translated twelve novels for Europa Editions and two books by Primo Levi for a new collected works from Norton. He also translates books for Harvard, Columbia, and Princeton university presses, and has written book reviews for the *Boston Globe*, the *Washington Post Book World*, and the *Journal of Modern Italian Studies*. Shugaar has a master of science degree from Columbia University's Graduate School of Journalism, a bachelor of arts from the University of California at Los Angeles, and a diploma superiore from the Università per Stranieri in Perugia.

Un Amico Italiano

· EAT, PRAY, LOVE IN ROME ·

∾

LUCA SPAGHETTI

Translated by
ANTONY SHUGAAR

PENGUIN BOOKS

PENGUIN BOOKS

Published by the Penguin Group

Penguin Group (USA) Inc., 375 Hudson Street, New York, New York 10014,
U.S.A. • Penguin Group (Canada), 90 Eglinton Avenue East, Suite 700, Toronto,
Ontario, Canada M4P 2Y3 (a division of Pearson Penguin Canada Inc.) • Penguin Books Ltd,
80 Strand, London WC2R 0RL, England • Penguin Ireland, 25 St Stephen's Green,
Dublin 2, Ireland (a division of Penguin Books Ltd) • Penguin Group (Australia),
250 Camberwell Road, Camberwell, Victoria 3124, Australia (a division of Pearson Australia
Group Pty Ltd) • Penguin Books India Pvt Ltd, 11 Community Centre, Panchsheel Park,
New Delhi – 110 017, India • Penguin Group (NZ), 67 Apollo Drive, Rosedale,
Auckland 0632, New Zealand (a division of Pearson New Zealand Ltd) • Penguin Books
(South Africa) (Pty) Ltd, 24 Sturdee Avenue, Rosebank, Johannesburg 2196, South Africa

Penguin Books Ltd, Registered Offices: 80 Strand, London WC2R 0RL, England

First published in Penguin Books 2011

3 5 7 9 10 8 6 4 2

Copyright © RCS Libri S.p.A., Milan, 2010
Translation copyright © Antony Shugaar, 2011
All rights reserved

Originally published in Italian as *Un romano per amico* by RCS Libri S.p.A., Milan.

LIBRARY OF CONGRESS CATALOGING IN PUBLICATION DATA
Spaghetti, Luca.
[Romano per amico. English]
Un amico italiano : eat, pray, love in Rome / Luca Spaghetti ; translated by Antony Shugaar.
p.   cm.
"Originally published in Italian as Un romano per amico
by RCS Libri S.p.A., Milan"—T.p. verso.
ISBN 978-0-14-311957-9
1. Spaghetti, Luca.   2. Travel agents—Italy.   3. Gilbert, Elizabeth, 1969—Travel.
4. Travel writers—United States.   5. Rome (Italy)—Description and travel.
6. Rome (Italy)   I. Title.
G154.5.S63 2011
914.504'93—dc22   2010054519

Printed in the United States of America
Set in Galliard
Designed by Elke Sigal

*Penguin is committed to publishing works of quality and integrity.
In that spirit, we are proud to offer this book to our readers;
however, the story, the experiences, and the words
are the author's alone.*

For Giorgio

Watch my back and light my way,
My traveling star, my traveling star.

—JAMES TAYLOR

Contents

Part Three

AN AMERICAN IN ROME

Introduction

❧

Believe It or Not

"*Among all the nominees on my Potential New Italian Friends List, I am most intrigued to meet a fellow named . . . brace yourself . . . Luca Spaghetti. And that is honestly his name, I swear to God, I'm not making it up. It's too crazy. I mean—just think of it. Anyhow, I plan to get in touch with Luca Spaghetti just as soon as possible.*"

Writing in 2003, Elizabeth Gilbert, the journalist and author, used those words to introduce one of the characters of her new book, *Eat, Pray, Love*, the true story of her yearlong journey of rebirth across Italy, India, and Indonesia, in search of herself and true love. That young man—whose name seemed like something out of a tourist brochure about Italy, who had driven her around Rome on the back of his beat-up scooter, dragged her to the stadium to watch Sunday soccer matches, and had taken her out to sample dishes that only a real Roman could love and appreciate—was me. And, yes—since you ask—I really do exist, and my last name really is Spaghetti. Born and raised in Rome, a self-taught guitarist, a devoted soccer fan, and a lover of good cooking. Until seven years ago, I had no idea of the adventure that lay before me. Because no one, much less me, could have imagined that *Eat, Pray, Love* would be translated into practically every language on earth, enchanting an incredible number of readers everywhere with its candor and irony and becoming a phenomenal international bestseller, with millions and millions of copies sold. But for me, Liz's book was simply the true—and therefore all the more remarkable—story of what happened when a blond American girl, pretty but unhappy, full of curiosity and love of life, came to Rome. I met her one September day, through a mutual friend, but in a short time she became one of the most important people in my life. A real friend, a friend I'll never forget.

How could I ever have imagined that, in any country I visited around the world, I'd find copies of Liz's books at the airport, or that my face would wind up on one of the most popular television shows in the United States, the *Oprah Winfrey Show*, where Liz would show the viewers a photograph of the two of us together in Rome? Who would have thought that readers from every walk of life and from around the world would ask me, curiously: Are you *the*

Luca Spaghetti? And last of all, who would have ever thought that the story would be made into a movie, with Julia Roberts playing my friend Liz? Or that I myself would be portrayed in that movie, played by a likable and jovial Italian actor.

Life is odd and full of surprises: Liz taught me that. And she taught me the value of true friendship, the kind of friendship that neither time nor distance can undermine. Friendship, as she and I have said to each other many times, is almost *a different kind of love*.

In this book, I've tried to tell my part of the story: my life, my dreams, my passions, my unexpected and extraordinary friendship with Liz, and the joys of my beloved birthplace, Rome. The Rome that I have known my whole life, since I was a child playing soccer in the courtyard, being made fun of for a surname that smacks of red checkered tablecloths and tomato sauce; the Rome that I explored inch by inch with Liz, sharing with her my loves and my memories—sharing my whole self, because that is how true friends are made—and in turn learning from her a valuable lesson about life and starting over, how you can always find the strength inside yourself to search, search, search, until you find what you're really looking for. And most important of all, I discovered that happiness can be hiding where you least expect it: in a plate of pasta with fresh tomatoes, in a goal scored by your beloved soccer team, in a glass of ice-cold wine in the Campo de' Fiori, in the excitement of learning a brand-new word in a language you're just beginning to know.

Because, as the great Roman poet Trilussa once wrote, in a poem entitled *Felicità*, "When you add it all up, happiness is a small thing."

Un Amico Italiano

Part One

ROMA, NUN FA' LA STUPIDA ...

1

⚛

That's Why I'm Here

My grandmother always used to tell me: "Your last name is going to bring you luck! When people meet you, it makes them happy. And a little bit hungry, too . . ."

Of course, I never believed her. I didn't understand what she meant. Every time she said it, I just thought she was making fun of me, like everyone else.

We were in Italy, in Rome—it must have been 1978 or so—and I was a child, a child whose mind was just beginning to register what it meant to have my last name: *Spaghetti*. It was an enormous burden to place on the fragile shoulders of a seven-year-old boy.

At first I hadn't fully grasped that it was my last name at all. It's probably just a nickname, I told myself. Maybe a few generations back we had a fat and jolly ancestor who ran a trattoria and was famous for his *spaghetti all'amatriciana*.

Or else, even before I was born, my father had made a name for himself by consuming an outlandish amount of pasta on one occasion or another, so impressing all his friends with his prowess as an eater that he earned himself that sobriquet.

It's true that when people asked me my name, I would say, "Luca Spaghetti," but only because my parents had told me that's what I should say.

It wasn't until I started school that the full meaning of my last name dawned on me. Or, what was worse, it dawned on my classmates. In first grade, the situation was still relatively peaceful, but every September in the years that followed, when classes resumed after the summer break, I dreaded the first roll call. When the teacher got to my name, the entire class would burst into laughter. But I was too young to be able to laugh at myself. As if that weren't bad enough, I had a little brother, Fabio Spaghetti, four years younger than me; naturally enough, I wanted to protect him from the same miserable fate. I did my best to warn him, but luckily for him, he hadn't yet grasped the gravity of the situation. I remember weighing the benefits of simply eliminating him entirely—I may even have made a few efforts in that direction. In my great and farsighted benevolence, I simply wanted to spare him the ordeal I was undergoing. My parents, unfortunately, failed to see things my way. They thought that my determination to wipe Fabio off the face of the earth was because I was "jealous of my little brother," not a result of "my great and farsighted benevolence." (Just for the record, let me point out that Fabio is alive and well, and he still carries our surname with pride.)

Of course, over time my classmates and my friends from the parish after-school program—where I went to play soccer every afternoon—gradually got used to my name, but still . . . For instance, whenever there was an argument, I always started out with a handicap. I got used to hearing the inevitable retort: "What do you know? Your name's Spaghetti!"

And that's not to mention the little rocket scientists who, at least once a week, would ring our buzzer, and when we asked over the intercom, "Who is it?," would shout, unfailingly, "Hey, Spaghetti—you want some tomato sauce?"

My mamma and papa, and my grandmother Ines, who lived with us, would simply smile at what they saw as nothing more than a harmless prank. To me, the situation was dire, intolerable. I had no recourse. What was I supposed to do? How could I retaliate against a kid my age named, let's say, Carlo Bianchi? (Bianchi, meaning "white," is the second most common family name in Italy.) Sing back, "Ciao, Mario Rossi says hello!"—a taunt based on Rossi ("red"), the most common family name in Italy? It wouldn't have the same sting.

Perhaps the root of the problem is the special relationship we Italians have with pasta. I've often wondered where this unconditional love springs from. It can't be just simple familiarity—the fact that at least once, often twice, a day this heaven-sent manna appears on our dining room tables, at lunch or dinner. There must be something more to it. In Italy, putting a steaming plate of *bucatini all'amatriciana* in front of someone who's just returned from a trip abroad is the finest welcome-back gesture you can make. How many times have I overheard phone calls made by compatriots who were returning from overseas? Their one and only concern is that, the minute they turn the front-door key, they see, in the distance—beyond the radiant faces of mother, wife, or whoever welcoming them home—the oversized pasta pot boiling on the stove.

According to the dictionary, I am—well, *spaghetti* is—"a type of long, thin pasta with a round cross section, a mainstay of Italian cuisine." That same dictionary goes on to define *pasta* as "a foodstuff made with bran or flour of various grains or seeds, divided into small regular shapes, and cooked in moist heat; it may also be used to describe a dish in which pasta is the chief ingredient, accompanied by a sauce or other flavoring." Make no mistake: if that's your last name, and you live in Italy, it's not something you can take lightly.

I've given quite a bit of thought to the question of what my favorite kind of pasta is. The knee-jerk answer is obvious: I love spaghetti . . . But I really ought to recuse myself from the running entirely. To even begin to answer this question, we need to agree on some classifications and categories. We'd have to distinguish between, for instance, long pasta and short pasta, smooth and ridged pasta, fresh pasta, homemade pasta, pasta with filling—and then we could add variants that, to my mind, don't really fall under the heading of pasta at all, such as lasagne and cannelloni, though they're often grouped in that category. But even then we can't really say that one kind of pasta is preferable to another, because the pivotal role is almost certainly played by the sauce or other flavorings.

This is my personal pasta ranking system: For long pasta—just the pasta itself without sauce—first place goes to spaghetti, obviously. (To be specific, spaghetti number 5.) But if we're talking about long pasta *with* sauce, then bucatini are unrivaled. Bucatini are like spaghetti, but thicker, and hollow, like a drinking straw. They have a wonderful, irresistible consistency—the sirloin steak of the pasta world—and each and every strand acts as a powerful sauce magnet. There is only one problem with bucatini, though: you can't possibly eat a plateful and stay clean. A bucatino is a natural sauce catapult. There are only two ways to approach a plate of bucatini without worrying about the tomato sauce that will inevitably fire off in all directions: either sit down for your meal stark naked, or wrap yourself up in napkins from head to toe like an Egyptian mummy (leaving your mouth free and ready for use, of course).

I've seen people shoot drops of pasta sauce over a distance of yards, hitting neighboring tables as they struggle to spin forkfuls of rebellious bucatini dripping with tomato. I've watched with amusement as a reckless diner orders bucatini during a business lunch, only to leave the restaurant with a once pristine, now polka-dot suit. And at weddings, I've been astonished at the sheer bravery (and folly) of newlyweds who insist on bucatini as the first course of their reception dinner, recklessly endangering not only the formal suits and gowns of their guests, but the bride's exquisite wedding dress.

Let's move on to the short pasta. As far as I'm concerned, there's no question that "ridged" short pasta is far superior to "smooth" short pasta. I love sauce, and I must tell you that, sadly, smooth pasta doesn't seem able to hold on to the sauce. Maybe this kind of pasta is better suited to people who prefer the taste of the noodle to the taste of the sauce. Ridged pasta, on the other hand, just seems to attract and hold sauce to its surface. Penne, rigatoni, macaroni, mezze maniche—each of these short pasta varieties has its own particular shape and size, and each was probably designed for a specific sauce. In fact, in Rome it is traditional to serve a specific sauce for every variety of noodle: *penne all'arrabbiata, rigatoni alla pajata,* and so on. A special case is the fusillo, with its peculiar corkscrew shape; it's technically a smooth pasta, but its unusual shape makes it behave very much like a ridged noodle.

Foreigners especially seem to love fettuccine with butter. Incredibly, the mere combination of an egg noodle— fettuccine, or, as we Italians say, *la fettuccina*—with butter is a marriage made in heaven. Of course, it's not as easy as it appears: apparently there is a technique for mixing the butter perfectly to create a sort of luxurious blend that ideally coats each individual fettuccina. Foreign visitors love it. We Romans, not so much . . . But at least once in our lives, we've all tasted this dish.

There are also specialties from each of Italy's twenty-one regions, pasta with special shapes accompanied by specific local sauces. These range from the *orecchiette alle cime di rapa* from Puglia to Ligurian *trofie al pesto*, and include as well Sardinian *spaghetti con la bottarga*, *pizzoccheri* from Lombardy's Valtellina, *strozzapreti* from Trentino, the *pici* of Tuscany, Sicily's *spaghetti alla norma* and *pasta con le sarde*, and—last but most certainly not least—Roman *cacio e pepe* served not in a bowl, but inside a hollowed wheel of Pecorino Romano cheese.

And then there is stuffed pasta, which attains its highest form of expression in tortellini, agnolotti, and, of course, ravioli. The tortellino may not be especially suited for innovative approaches: it seems to do best in a traditional setting, served in a broth or a meat sauce. With ravioli, a problem usually arises with the portion, especially when you're dining out. Everyone loves ravioli, especially kids, but when you order ravioli in a restaurant, you generally wind up with a dispiriting little pile of three, maybe four rectangles placed in front of you. Four is the most you can expect to get here in Italy, if the chef is feeling generous that day, but there's no hoping for a higher number. I'm serious. It's scarcely enough individual ravioli to get the flavor. They tell the story in Rome about a guy who orders a dish of ravioli. When the waiter brings his order, he looks down with some irritation at the desolate loneliness of three little ravioli in the middle of the plate. He spears all three ravioli—lining them up on a single forkful—and gulps them down all at once. Then he turns to the waiter, who is hovering nearby, and says, in the distinctive Roman accent: "*Bboni, mo' puoi butta' in pentola l'altri trenta!*"— These were good, now how about tossing the other thirty into the pot!

But let's talk about the *primi*—the first course, which is almost always pasta—specific to Rome. In this city, pasta is serious business: *spaghetti alla carbonara, alla gricia, all'aglio olio e peperoncino, al cacio e pepe,* or *bucatini all'amatriciana, rigatoni con la pajata, pasta e fagioli, fettuccine alla papalina, gnocchi alla romana* . . . That's not all of them, but it's a respectable start. These are dishes that epitomize, with their simplicity and their humble ingredients, the heart and soul of Roman cooking. Some of these dishes have the added value of being supremely easy to prepare, such as *pasta cacio e pepe,* or else *aglio olio e peperoncino*—with garlic, olive oil, and chili peppers. That makes them especially beloved by us Roman men. All it takes is a pot of boiling water and the normal pasta cooking time, and you look like a master chef!

The wonderful underlying characteristic of pasta is that nobody doesn't like it. Disarmingly simple, easy and quick to make, it's an ideal solution for each and every person, season, and occasion. It lends itself to every flavor combi-

nation imaginable, it satisfies vegetarians as well as carni-
vores, and it welcomes both fresh, cheerful sauces in the
summer and substantial, warming sauces in the winter. It
can even be an erotic accompaniment for lovers spending
the evening in. Admittedly, there are fine points of disagreement concerning tastes and preferences, cooking
times and techniques for preparation, but these are argu-
ments that—unlike the ones we have to put up with on a
daily basis—bring joy, a gleam to the eye, and lip-smacking
anticipation.

It's the same kind of anticipation that my surname seems
to arouse. I'd like to know if there is someone named Franz
Kartoffeln in Germany, or a John Hamburger in America, a
Nikos Souvlaki in Greece, or Brigitte Baguette in France; I
also wonder if these folks would have the same effect on
people's appetites and moods. We would make a wonderful
team—maybe the five of us couldn't solve world hunger,
but we'd certainly expect to be given seats on the executive
board of the UN's Food and Agriculture Organization.

At any rate, as I grew up, my surname became increasingly likable and less and less the target of ridicule. My
friends played fewer stupid pranks. Though other problems arose. Girls, to name just one!

Competition between boys in the age range of ten to
twelve can be murderous. Being rejected by a little girl that
age whom you've asked to be your girlfriend, your *fidan-
zatina*, can throw you into the depths of preadolescent
depression. Admittedly, the whole ordeal might span no

more than three or four hours, but it would still leave deep marks on one's unfortunate ego. I started to wonder, would there ever be a girl in this world willing to consider marrying a boy named Spaghetti? And even if she didn't take his last name, would she be willing to have kids with him? A family of Spaghettini? (I should step in here and point out that spaghettini are not only the children of two spaghetti, but also a pasta format with a respectable history, similar in every way to spaghetti proper but slightly smaller in diameter, and the absolute best medium, if cooked perfectly al dente, for a fresh tomato and basil sauce.) She probably wouldn't. Unless, of course, her surname was already Tagliatella.

So, as you can see, life for a Spaghetti starts out with its challenges.

2

❧

Places in My Past

*T*here's no point in concealing the fact: I'm a Roman and proud of it. Even though being a Spaghetti is probably worse in Rome than it would be anywhere else in Italy.

That's because the inhabitants of Rome have a very particular sense of humor. The fact is that the Roman sense of humor is unrivaled, and we Romans grow up with the unshakable belief that irony is a crucial part of living well. A purebred Roman knows not to take people or situations too seriously, and whenever possible, he tries to make fun of them, in the wonderfully exaggerated and jocular manner that we Romans are famous for. I don't know many people in Rome who really get worked up about trivial problems. Of course, the world is full of touchy people—unquestionably—but if you had to rank the places in Italy according to uptightness, you might find Rome near the bottom of the list. You wouldn't survive long here other-wise. Maybe you weren't born with this particular gift of jocularity, but if you're paying attention, you figure it out at a pretty young age. It's a bit like having to figure out which side you're on in terms of your soccer team—are you root-ing for S.S. Lazio or A.S. Roma? Otherwise, life becomes too difficult, so it's better to come to terms with it early.

In fact, the mocking, humorous tone prevails in Rome. You can find it everywhere. Even in the signs on the shops and cafés: Grazie a Dio È Venerdì and Qua Nun Se More Mai are both restaurants proclaiming, respectively, Thank God It's Friday and Here, You Never Die; Mai di Lunedì, Diamoci un Taglio, Doppie Punte—Never on Monday, Cut It Out, and Split Ends are hairdressers; Da 0 a 4 Zampe is a pet store offering From Zero to Four Legs; Che Te Ce Metto?, meaning What Do You Want on It?, is a *paninoteca*, or sandwich shop. The idea there may be to encourage people to be ready with their order before even coming inside.

We try not to take things too seriously on the job, ei-ther. There's that old saying: Never put off till tomorrow what you can do today. We Romans, on the other hand, find Mark Twain's version more persuasive: "Never put off until tomorrow what you can do the day after tomor-row." First of all, though, let me make one thing clear. Some people think that Romans aren't very interested in work—that's just one of the many stereotypes about the capital of Italy. But the reality is actually quite different. In

Rome, in fact, we work hard, but the good thing is that we know how to distribute in a very strategic manner the time we spend working and the time we spend relaxing. For instance, we tend to take it easy in the morning, building up in a relaxed manner to the grueling day that lies ahead of us . . . There are various approaches: for example, we'll read the newspaper because it's a good thing to be well informed, or else we'll have a second cup of coffee, either out at a café or from the office coffee machine. Later, we might take advantage of our lunch break for a long workout at the gym, without giving up a hot meal, either at the gym's cafeteria or at a lunch place along the way—completely nullifying the effects of the exercise, so you start over from scratch the next day. And if you're not particularly athletic, then the most popular destination is any restaurant, for lunch complete with *primo*, *secondo*, side dish, dessert, espresso, and—of course—*ammazzacaffè*, the exquisitely dubbed "coffee-killer," a liqueur to end the meal on a glorious note. And in fact there are restaurants and trattorias in certain quarters of Rome, such as Prati or Parioli, that are busier at lunch than dinner. So we Romans like to distribute our time the way it suits us best, in part because you can always catch up in the evening. We tend to work late, making up for the morning's or afternoon's "distractions." The secret is to remain calm, dealing with problems one at a time, taking care to keep the stress at bay.

But it is the beauty of Rome that most distracts us from

our work: this city possesses an unrivaled artistic patri-
mony, and even though we often overlook it as we zip past
on our scooters or walk down into the underground stations of our Metropolitana transit system, every so often
we stop, breathless, astonished at the city's beauty. One
day there might be an unusual shade of sunlight on the
Forum, or we might happen to glance over at the unruf-
fled waters of the Tiber as it flows past, or we'll notice how
the change of seasons makes the Eternal City change with
them: the winter, aromatic with chestnuts roasting over
open fires, makes way for spring evenings in the cafés of
Trastevere; the *grattachecche*—grated ice and fruit juices—
made in kiosks are the flavor of summer holidays, and September sunsets, arriving a little earlier each day, alert us
that autumn is at the city gates.

There are lots of places in Rome that conceal mysterious
histories, and I like to tell those backstories to my foreign
friends when they come to visit me, or even to friends who
don't happen to know them even though they've lived
their whole lives in Rome.

The hospital of Santo Spirito, on the banks of the Tiber
near the Castel Sant'Angelo, with all the history that it
boasts, is certainly one of these places. First of all, it's one of
the oldest hospitals in Europe, which is enough to give you
goose bumps, if you stop to think about it. But the most

interesting thing about it is that, according to legend, what drove Pope Innocent III to build a hospital on the banks of the Tiber, to shelter the sick and the elderly as well as abandoned children, was a dream he'd had. In his dream, an angel denounced the crimes of mothers who threw their unwanted newborn infants into the waters of Rome's river. This is the origin of the *rota*—or wheel—still visible to the left of the monumental Baroque portal in the Borgo Santo Spirito. It harks back to the age-old tradition of the "wheel of the foundlings." From the exterior, in order to ensure the anonymity of those abandoning their little ones, illegitimate children could be submitted to the care of the prioress. The left foot of each foundling was marked with a double cross. Later they could be once again set out in the wheel for potential adoption. Each foundling was registered as *filius m. ignotae*—in Latin, "son of unknown mother," with the *m* standing for *matris*. In time, the common folk of Rome, overlooking the period following the letter *m*, began to condense the phrase in everyday speech into *filius mignotae*, hence the pejorative term *mignotta*, used fairly frequently in the city. So if you happen to attend a soccer match in Rome, more often than not you'll hear that phrase used, usually to describe the female parent of the referee.

And how could I ever resist telling the story of one of my favorite Roman monuments: the Trevi Fountain, a destination for tourists but also for any teenage Roman out on an unsupervised excursion. The fountain itself dates back to ancient times, as it was the terminus of the Aqua Virgo, the aqueduct that Marcus Vipsanius Agrippa built in Rome in 19 BC to supply water for the city's baths. The name of the spring, Aqua Virgo, derives from the legend according to which a young girl, or *virgo* in Latin, showed Agrippa the location of the spring. And so, Agrippa set up one of the lesser fountains of the aqueduct, with three collection basins, in what we now call the Piazza di Trevi. Through a succession of construction projects and restorations, those humble collection basins became the magnificent fountain that now fills the piazza. It was in the first half of the seventeenth century, under Pope Urban VIII, that the fountain began to take its current shape. The pope had decided to make it a magnificent monument, and to that end he hired the sculptor and architect Gian Lorenzo Bernini. Bernini presented a series of plans, all of them very expensive, to the point that the pope had to raise taxes in order to finance them—specifically, the tax on wine, for which the Barberini pope would go down in history:

In order to ensure the Roman water supply
Pope Urban did a wine tax apply.

Urban VIII and Bernini both died before the fountain could be completed; Niccolò Salvi finished the job in the eighteenth century.

Among the legends that circulate about this famous

fountain, the best-known one claims that by turning your back on the fountain and then tossing in a coin, you are sure to return to Rome. Less well known but certainly more intriguing is the story about the large vase on the right side of the fountain, nicknamed the "Ace of Cups" because of its resemblance to the ace of the Italian deck of cards. It is said that it was placed there to thwart the heckling of a barber whose shop was on that side of the fountain. The barber had been very critical of Bernini's project, and the vase was erected in order to block his view of construction. Maybe that shut him up once and for all. Of course, if he had ever imagined that one day a statuesque beauty like Anita Ekberg might go for a wade in the fountain by the light of the moon, maybe he would have been more accepting . . .

Another place I like to visit, and especially enjoy taking visitors, is the Church of Sant'Ignazio di Loyola—or St. Ignatius Loyola. Every time I do, I enjoy waiting to see how long it takes my guests to notice that the dome of the church is a fake—and many never notice at all. In fact, the interior of the dome is a magnificent *trompe l'oeil* painting by Andrea Pozzo positioned over the vault of the church, designed in such a way that it creates an optical illusion: the eye sees the canvas as an actual dome. There's a mark on the floor near the altar indicating the best place to stand to view the fake dome. Apparently it was a genius alternative devised by the painter when a shortage of funds made it impossible to build the majestic masonry cupola called for in his initial plans. Andrea Pozzo was a past master of the art of perspectival illusion. It is wonderful to stand before his works, such as the hallway in the Stanze di Sant'Ignazio in the Chiesa del Gesù, and see how long it takes to see that they are actually much smaller than they appear at first sight.

St. Peter's Square, too, has a number of tricks it plays on the eye of the visitor. Among them, the two "centers of the colonnade" are especially popular with children. The piazza is oval in shape, but it's an oval actually made up of two semicircles, each lined by a colonnade consisting of four rows of columns. It's possible to distinguish the separate rows of columns from any point in the piazza, except when you stand in either of the two centers of the colonnade. For each semicircle, there is one point—the center of the colonnade—from which the rows of columns line up perfectly, the four columns collapsing into just one. For us kids who grew up in the neighborhood around St. Peter's, the centers of the colonnade were the principal attraction of the city, and we loved to show them off to tourists or friends visiting Rome. More than once, I have to confess, we used them as landmarks for an improvised soccer field in St. Peter's Square. Before the attempted assassination of Pope John Paul II in 1981, in fact, there were no barriers or security systems in place in St. Peter's Square. So when a group of small boys showed up equipped with the requisite soccer ball, it was difficult to resist the allure of such a wide-open public space. And when the guards on duty suggested we might want to go back to play in the courtyard of our local parish church, they seemed to be particularly concerned that we might disturb the afternoon nap of His Holiness and less worried that we were using one of the most sacred and touristed places on earth as if it were our own personal Maracanã Stadium.

Another place with more than a few surprises in store is the Aventino, one of the seven hills of ancient Rome and very arguably the loveliest. It looms over the Circus Maximus and its slopes are graced by Rome's magnificent municipal rose garden, the Roseto Comunale. Atop the hill are perched the beautiful and charming medieval churches of Sant'Anselmo, Sant'Alessio, and Santa Sabina. It is hard to count the number of weddings that have been celebrated up here—there's a wedding every day of the year! Moreover, this is one of the best places in Rome for courtship and wooing, especially if you sneak off to the wonderful Giardino degli Aranci, or Orange Garden, another charming and romantic spot on my favorite Roman hill.

But the main reason I loved the Aventino when I was a child was the Piazza dei Cavalieri di Malta—the Piazza of the Knights of Malta—where the military order of that name had its headquarters, in a building with a majestic entrance that was always locked tight. But the massive doors have a keyhole, and it's always a surprise and a delight to look through it. If you happen to be passing by, it's irresistible to take a peek. The doorway—bolted and locked—

seems to be there for that sole purpose: just so that anyone who wishes can peer through the keyhole, without embarrassment, without feeling you're engaging in something illicit, and without anyone saying a thing to you about it. And there's nothing frightening or unseemly on the other side of that door—just one of the most magnificent views Rome has to offer. A long tree-lined drive, with branches reaching out to intertwine overhead, creates a magnificent perspective of arches and depth, leading directly to the dome of St. Peter's, visible in the distant background.

I still remember my astonishment when I was taken to see it for the first time as a child. I was terrified to peep through the keyhole because my parents had always told me that's something you shouldn't do, and I was frightened at the idea of what I might see. But when I glimpsed this marvelous sight, my youthful eye was glued to that keyhole and the extraordinary spectacle that lay beyond. Since that day, this view holds a special place in my heart, and I try to make sure that if a friend hasn't seen it before, I take him or her there. I love to watch my friends' reactions: at first timid, and then gradually ecstatic. It's an unforgettable gift. In return, I have the image of their overjoyed faces filled with astonishment and wonder.

The thing about Rome is that it always manages to give you something special. There's always a hint of magic, be it something as simple as peering furtively in to admire the front hall of an ancient palazzo, or looking up to glimpse the wooden-beamed ceilings of apartments from the street, or just breathing in the mingled scents of wax candles and incense in a church you visit for the first time. Even stopping for a quick and refreshing drink from the *nasoni*, Rome's distinctive nose-shaped curved brass drinking fountains that dot the streets, can be a pure and simple joy.

It's true that for us Romans a stroll through the streets usually involves hidden lanes and nooks and little shops that tourists overlook, rather than the Colosseum or the Pantheon. That's not to say that from time to time we don't enjoy touring—*again* (which is to say, for the umpteenth time in our lives)—the Colosseum or the Pantheon, but sipping an espresso in a half-hidden little piazza, as spring blossoms all around you, under the world-weary eyes of a cat stretching out comfortably nearby . . . well, that's a whole different kind of pleasure.

Rome is all this, but also much more. It's a city with a thousand faces, but to a Roman, it is, quite simply: *Roma*.

Admittedly, Rome has other names and attributes: the Eternal City, *caput mundi* (in Latin, "capital of the world"), the cradle of modern civilization. And even though every Roman has had these ideas drummed into his heart and mind from infancy, we often choose to forget them.

Say that destiny decrees you are born in Arizona,

or Chile, or India, or else in Haiti, the Virgin Islands, the Netherlands. You could be born into any of a thousand other places. But if destiny decides you are to be born in Italy, and then narrows it down even further to—exceptionally—Rome, at a certain point in your life you start to feel that being born in Chile or India wouldn't have been exactly the same thing for you. But not for the obvious reasons. In fact, you can pretend it's nothing special until you're a teenager. You can keep on playing soccer, kicking the ball against the ancient city's Aurelian Walls near the Porta Metronia—the walls are only two thousand years old, but you don't know that yet. But as an adult, how can you pretend to be unimpressed when, after a full hour in a slowly moving line of cars, bumping over the *sampietrino* cobblestones, roughly as old as the walls, it dawns on you that for the past twenty years you've been "using" the Colosseum more or less as a traffic median? Or that—today like any other day—disgusted at the delay the traffic has caused, making you late for your business meeting, you haven't even noticed the wealth of history that surrounds you on all sides?

At a certain point in your life, you understand that—quite simply—you happen to have been born in the most beautiful city on earth. And you think back, in no particular order, to everything it's given you. You think back to the excursions you took as a child to the "beaches of Rome," at Ostia, and you remember your astonishment at the fact that the shoreline—mile after mile of sand and the unspoiled, sweet-smelling Mediterranean—should be so close to your home and the deafening noise of the city. You think back to your first outings on a motor scooter, when you rode through the city without your parents' permission and it seemed as if it would never come to an end. Maybe it was springtime, and the light of Rome was simply splendid, and it beckoned you to venture out into the meadows that line the Appia Antica—the ancient Appian Way—or toward the Roman Forum, a perfect place to snuggle in private with your first girlfriend. If nothing else, it was a place where no one would ever think to come looking for you.

If you think back to your first evenings out in Rome, get-togethers in the Via dei Fori Imperiali—a street named after the forums of the Roman empire, where ancient Roman nobles must have made appointments to meet in their chariots—you remember that one of the reasons it was so popular was that there was plenty of room to play soccer. Because—and you smile as you think back on this detail—there was always someone who'd show up with a soccer ball in the trunk of his car. Those evenings always ended in Trastevere, where you bought slices of pizza— Roman pizza, flat and crunchy—to eat in the narrow lanes off of white paper napkins.

And you look back on the things you've done since you were a boy, things you still do today: eating *cornetti* (the Italian equivalent of a croissant, with some variations) in the middle of the night in Vicolo del Cinque in Trastevere, or in the Testaccio area; at least once a year seeing the masterpieces of Caravaggio, who wasn't Roman by birth but who was happy to live in this city—*Vocazione di San Matteo* at the Church of San Luigi dei Francesi and the *Madonna di Loreto* in the Church of Sant'Agostino; standing in line for ten minutes to get an espresso, only to toss it back in thirty seconds, at the Bar Sant'Eustachio near the Pantheon; marveling at the majesty of St. Peter's, but also going there simply to hear Mass on a Sunday; amusing yourself by reading the improvised sonnets left by passersby at the statue of Pasquin, a variety of "Pasquinades" that rail against the current government, whatever its complexion, left wing, right wing, or middle of the road—no matter what, it's in the wrong; and driving past the Pyramid of Cestius, which may be just a small-scale imitation of the pyramids of Nubia, but it does date all the way back to 12 BC. And to think that nearby, in the Protestant Cemetery, the mortal remains of John Keats and Percy Bysshe Shelley, Antonio Gramsci and Carlo Emilio Gadda are buried. Or passing the time chatting with the usual waiter in the usual trattoria in the usual working-class neighborhood on the outskirts of Rome, where as usual you order *spaghetti alla carbonara,* which, like most Roman cooking, may not be easy to digest but—let's be honest—is better here than anywhere else on earth.

Places in My Past

Lost in the meandering memories of your past, you relive them every day in the unchanging present, and you decide that, even if in the years to come you do go on using the Colosseum as a traffic median—and an excellent one at that—you were certainly lucky to have been born in Rome.

3

Anywhere Like Heaven

*O*ne day, during Sunday Mass in a small church near my house, as the priest read from the Gospel in a strange language midway between Spanish and Italian, I found myself thinking: *How many churches are there in Rome?*

Out of curiosity, I researched it on the Internet. I never did find an exact number, though one crazy person said that he had counted them all one by one and he'd come up with 230 churches.

Given the size of Rome's historic center, it's difficult to answer the question with any confidence—even if you've lived in Rome your whole life, and even if you've spent a good portion of that life visiting churches, either dragged there by your parents or else while taking friends visiting Rome out sightseeing.

While you're out wandering around the city, there's

one church you really can't avoid seeing now and again, like it or not: *er Cupolone*, as we Romans affectionately call it—the Big Dome. In fact, St. Peter's Basilica in the Vatican, built on the spot where the apostle Peter is buried, is not only a symbol of Rome around the world, it's also an old friend for us Romans, a reassuring touchstone.

Many years ago, before terrorism became a lurking source of fear—and before you had to pass through a metal detector in order to enter St. Peter's—any time you strolled through the city at night you always seemed to wind up, for some reason, in the very center of the immense square designed and built by Bernini. And each time, unfailingly, you experienced the same strange sensation: you felt tiny in the presence of such a majestic creation. St. Peter's is, in fact, enormous—the largest Catholic church on earth. Until recently, there was an unwritten rule that no building should approach *er Cupolone* in height, much less outdo it. Times change, though, and now skyscrapers are being built even in Rome . . .

St. Peter's is, of course, the worldwide center of Catholicism. It's an impressive thought, even if you're not religious. It's practically impossible to list all the wondrous treasures it contains: marble busts, statues, tombs, tapestries, paintings, frescoes, mosaics, stuccoes. But when you walk into the basilica, the first thing you notice is the little crowd of people on your right. That's where the *Pietà* is located, which in my opinion is the most beautiful, tragic, and deeply human piece of sculpture on earth, carved by Michelangelo when he was barely twenty-four years old. The sculpture is now protected by a sheet of bulletproof glass, and has been since 1972, when a lunatic attacked it with a hammer and damaged it in several places.

In my own pilgrimages—not to holy places, but to the beaches outside Rome—I always seem to happen upon the basilica of San Paolo Fuori le Mura (literally, St. Paul Outside the Walls), which was built on what is traditionally thought to be the grave of St. Paul. It's located along the Via Ostiense, near the banks of the Tiber River. This section of riverbank is now lined with famous restaurants and clubs, like the one where the famous Italian author Pier Paolo Pasolini had dinner the night he was murdered. Whenever I'm in that part of town, I try to stop by a spot we Romans like to refer to as the Three Fountains, a couple of miles from the basilica. It's a complex of three churches and a monastery in a peaceful location just a short distance from the busy and noisy Roman thoroughfare Via Laurentina. There's an interesting reason for the name Three Fountains. It was on this spot that St. Paul was beheaded in AD 67. According to legend, his head bounced three times, and each time, on the spot where it hit, a spring of water gushed from the soil. Those three springs, or fountains, are now commemorated by the three churches. The oldest building, the monastery, was founded in AD 625 and occupied by Greek, Benedictine, and Cistercian monks, in that order. The spread of malaria drove the occupants away, and the monastery was entrusted to the Trappist Fathers, who planted eucalyptus trees, which were thought to ward off malaria. Miraculously, even now, many centuries later, the Trappists still produce a eucalyptus-based liqueur from those trees, which they sell in a little shop in the courtyard, along with their famous chocolate and a variety of herbal remedies. The place is steeped in silence and greenery, a wonderful oasis of peace far from the traffic and clamor of the city.

Another astonishing story that my father used to tell me when I was small concerns Santa Maria Maggiore (St. Mary Major), the other papal basilica. It was built on the site where, according to local lore, a heavy and absolutely miraculous snowfall occurred on August 4, in AD 352.

A patrician aristocrat named Joannes decided, since he was childless and with the agreement of his wife, to donate all his possessions to the church and to build a basilica dedicated to the Virgin Mary. Legend has it that the Madonna appeared to the couple during the night of August 4 in AD 352, telling them that a miracle would point to the best location on which to build their church. The pope had the exact same dream, and the following day, when he walked out onto the Esquiline Hill, he found it covered with snow. He traced out the perimeter of the building on the spot in the snow. When the church was built, at the couple's expense, it was known as the Church of St. Mary ad Nives—St.

Mary of the Snows; what we see today in Santa Maria Maggiore, though, is a reconstruction dating from a later period. The Madonna della Neve—Our Lady of the Snows—is a holiday celebrated throughout Italy on August 5. She is the patron saint of some forty Italian cities and towns. And every year in August, it rains white petals in Rome. What would Bernini, buried in the basilica of Santa Maria Maggiore, think of it?

With all this abundant excess of churches, it should come as no surprise that people in Rome, more than elsewhere, use an expression that involves no fewer than seven: the famous *giro delle sette chiese*—the circuit of the seven churches. When Romans talk about "making the circuit of the seven churches," they are evoking the idea of going the long way around, or making a circuitous detour before managing to achieve something. It was only after I grew up that I happened to ask myself what the seven churches in question might be and why every Roman, including me, refers to them from time to time. I discovered that the circuit of the seven churches actually was an ancient pilgrimage "circuit." St. Philip Neri decreed in 1540 that a pilgrim visiting Rome should pray in no fewer than seven churches, the main ecclesiastical institutions of the time, on a single day, Good Friday . . . and of course the only way to do that was on foot! I challenge you to find me even one Roman who has visited all seven of them, even once, in the course of a lifetime—much less on foot, rather than by car.

And just which seven churches are they? Aside from the four patriarchal basilicas—that is, St. Peter's, St. John Lateran, St. Paul Outside the Walls, and St. Mary Major—there were St. Lawrence Outside the Walls, near the Verano monumental cemetery, the Holy Cross in Jerusalem, and lastly St. Sebastian Outside the Walls, near the catacombs of St. Sebastian, not far from the Appia Antica.

But Rome has its modern churches as well. One winter Sunday I satisfied my curiosity about one of them. A few years ago, there had been quite a firestorm of controversy over the design and construction of a new church in an outlying working-class section of Rome, Tor Tre Teste. The city government had hired a big name in contemporary architecture, Richard Meier, to design and build it. Meier had won a sort of competition well ahead of the Great Jubilee of 2000, and the cornerstone was laid in 1998; however, the Jubilee Church, also known as the Church of God Our Merciful Father, was not completed until well after the Jubilee, in 2003. It is, to use the Italian expression, a *cattedrale nel deserto*, a "cathedral in the desert," located in the middle of a dense and fairly anonymous urban quarter. Meier, who also designed the controversial travertine and glass shell that contains the Ara Pacis—the emperor Augustus's Altar of Peace—on the banks of the Tiber, has created an impressive and intriguing building: three enormous, self-supporting white concrete vaults, the highest of the three reaching up eighty-five feet. Direct sunlight never penetrates the interior of the church, save for a single moment in the afternoon, when a shaft of light angles through a small window, illuminating the crucifix inside.

What can I say? It's a lovely church. But when I think back to St. Peter's and the most famous dome on earth . . .

4

Long Ago and Far Away

$\mathcal{W}$hat I've described to you so far is the Rome that every Roman gets to know as he grows up and comes to appreciate the beauties and the treasures that his city has to offer. But as a child, little Luca Spaghetti had very different interests.

The centerpiece in the life of every Italian *bambino* is probably Sunday. In fact, I remember the Sundays of my childhood as a succession of celebrations, in the sense that almost everything that happened on Sunday struck me as a special event. Saturday nights I would drop off to sleep already dreaming of awakening the following day, because that meant one thing that never happened during the week: I'd get to play soccer in the morning.

Of course, before I could unleash my energy and virtuoso soccer skills on the parish church's *pozzolana* ash soccer field, one obligatory rite of passage for every child on Sunday morning was Holy Mass at ten a.m.—a Mass held especially for the children. To be honest, we would happily have skipped the Mass, considering our yearning to play, but we basically underwent the ritual in a fairly good-natured manner. If nothing else, it was one way for all the junior soccer players to get together at a specific time near the field. There was another benefit: since we all sat together in the pews, during the homily we could already get started on the crucial task of dividing up into teams.

Once Mass was over, we gave free rein to our obsession with soccer, and a horde of yelling children surged onto a parish soccer field that was certainly far too small to accommodate all of us—because every child that had attended Mass had the right to play in the soccer match, even if they were terrible soccer players. And so the Sunday match involved rows of midget players, as many as thirty to a side. As if that weren't enough, each of us wore a jersey of a different color.

When the referee whistled the start of play, the army of midget players rushed off in pursuit of the soccer ball like a swarm of crazed bees. The soccer ball was usually a Super Tele, a round piece of plastic that behaved more or less like a kite in even a light breeze—completely impossible to control. Ricochets and rebounds were unpredictable on a soccer field that had pitfalls of all kinds: plane trees forty feet tall along the foul lines; depressions, boulders, and hills that made the terrain varied and treacherous. There was also a tremendous low limestone wall about a foot tall around the field. Behind one goal with rusted uprights there was a fifteen-foot-high wall; behind the other goal, with even rustier uprights, there was a very tall net that was evidently meant to protect the windows of the neighboring houses. That's what it was *supposed* to do, anyway . . .

I remember games in which I never got to touch the ball at all: all I managed to do was get a mouthful of dust kicked up by the other players as they skidded and swerved across the *pozzolana* ash with moves worthy of Wile E. Coyote and Road Runner. As often as not, once the swarm of players had overrun me, I would stand—or lie—there, counting the fallen bodies of the other injured players as the dirt cloud dissipated.

Some of the players, more ruthless and less willing to work hard than the others, would simply line up along the opposing team's goal, trusting in blind fate to arrange for the ball to roll or bounce, by chance, to their feet, so they could then turn and quickly, easily score a goal. When that happened, the celebrations would go on for as long as fifteen minutes, and it became quite a challenge to get the game started again.

These games usually ended when the parents showed up, one after another, to take their sons home, or when that week's referee officially decreed it was time for lunch.

Lunchtime, of course, was fundamental. Around one

o'clock, the children all scattered down the various streets of our neighborhood, hurrying the short distance home. During the trip, I always looked longingly at the wonderful, mouthwatering sign of the neighborhood pastry shop, because Sunday lunch always involved pastries—what we called *pastarelle*. There was always a long line in the pastry shop, because everyone always hurried in just before one o'clock to make sure they would enjoy the privilege of buying pastries from the last batch, and also to make sure the *pastarelle* didn't sit too long in the refrigerator at home. There is a long-standing and contentious debate about the best *pastarella* format. Some are in favor of the *mignon*. Those who prefer that smaller format may just be especially gluttonous for sweets, and so they like to be able to sample the largest number of varieties, under the illusion that they're limiting their intake of calories. Then there are those—like me—who prefer the large format, the true *pastarella*. When you take your first bite, there is an unmistakable explosion of cream filling in your mouth. No one can resist the *pastarella*, even people who aren't especially fond of sweets, and the pastries we ate on Sundays really did have the flavor of a special occasion.

After we left the pastry shop, there was one more aroma that reminded me that I was consumed with a ravenous hunger following the soccer game: the scent of meat sauce bubbling on the stove, wafting out of nearly every window: *il ragù della domenica*—the Sunday meat sauce. Though I've never really been clear on how it's spelled—*ragù, ra-*

gout, or *ragou*—whatever the spelling, it definitely stimulates the appetite all the same.

Now, we weren't in Naples and we weren't in Bologna, the two great centers of Italian meat sauce, but still, we know what we're doing in Rome when it comes to *ragù*. Nowadays, perhaps, the tradition is being lost, but in Italy *ragù* has always been the classic Sunday specialty for various reasons. One of the main reasons is the time it takes to make it, and an Italian mother finds that extra time only on the seventh day of the week. The second consideration is the sheer cost of making meat sauce: *ragù* every day would bankrupt Bill Gates. And that's to say nothing of digestibility: not many people would be able to go back to work in the afternoon after piling on a healthy helping of *fettuccine al ragù* for lunch.

The traditional Spaghetti family recipe is as follows: In a few tablespoons of oil, sauté ground beef, along with lard, pancetta (similar but not identical to American bacon), parsley, pepper, finely chopped garlic, and onions. When the meat is nicely browned, lower the flame and start pouring in wine little by little, letting it evaporate, and then adding more until the components in the saucepan are evenly mixed. At this point, add crushed tomatoes and continue sautéing, stirring constantly, until the sauce has turned a very dark red. This process requires a very long cooking time, and actually demands an even longer resting time, so that the ingredients can blend together to perfection. There are even people who make a *ragù* the previous day, so that it will be ready and "rested" for their Sunday lunch.

When it came time to scoop up the last driblets of sauce in the bowl, we were always well supplied with bread purchased directly from the baker's oven in Trastevere. After the *scarpetta* (literally, "little shoe"), as we call this bowl-cleaning ritual, we were all ready to dive into the *secondo*, which was generally an *involtino*, or roulade, thin slices of meat rolled up with a stuffing of garlic, cheese, salt, and pepper, and then fastened together with a pair of toothpicks and browned in a saucepan with oil and garlic and the usual addition of white wine and tomatoes. There it was, an extra blast of nutrition, just in case the *ragù* proved insufficient.

Before reemerging to enjoy the remaining amusements Sunday had to offer, I, for one, had to undertake one last act that was fairly challenging for a child my age: crossing the street, as I lived on the Via Gregorio VII, a long thoroughfare that runs straight to St. Peter's Square. After lunch on a Sunday, there was a constant flow of pedestrians, tour buses, and cars coming back from the Angelus prayer, which the pope recited every Sunday at noon.

I don't know how many times I walked down Via Gregorio VII to go to St. Peter's, but I do remember one time in particular, when Karol Wojtyła was elected pope as John Paul II. The whole city turned out for the event, even a multitude of non-Catholics, because in Rome the pope is ultimately considered a sort of benevolent old uncle—a member of the family, in other words. Many times, in the years that followed, I sat there on my scooter, held up by the city traffic cops, the *vigili,* even though the traffic light was green, in order to allow the pope's motorcade through. It is always fun to see the expressions of amazement on the faces of the tourists standing at the stoplight when I explain, "The pope is about to go by!" Their helpless, astonished faces always make me feel slightly protective of them.

The election of John Paul II was deeply moving for me. My parents had explained that I could understand the outcome of the vote from the color of the puffs of smoke that issued from the little chimney above the Sistine Chapel: a puff of black smoke if none of the candidates had yet received the requisite two-thirds of the votes of the College of Cardinals, or a puff of white smoke if a new pontiff had been elected. The black smoke came when they burned the ballots from the unsuccessful election; the white smoke was generated by tossing damp straw into the oven.

Caught up in the infectious excitement of the people all around me in the immensity of St. Peter's Square, I never took my eyes off the chimney, hoping I'd see a puff of white smoke. Instead, however, after a long, long wait, a dreary puff of black smoke, accompanied by a collective *Oohhhh* of disappointment from the crowd, informed us that they had been unsuccessful. I asked my parents whether the conclave might remain in session a little longer, if they might not think it over and elect a pope before going to sleep; that way, at school the next day I could boast that *I'd been there*. They explained to me that electing a pope wasn't as simple and straightforward as tossing a couple of sausages on the grill. So we walked back home along the slight uphill slope of Via Gregorio VII. I was only able to see the eventual puff of white smoke on television; likewise the first speech of John Paul II.

Of course, for the papal Angelus on an ordinary Sunday, there was none of the oceanic crowd that stood in St. Peter's Square expectantly awaiting the election of a new pope. Still, we had to be very cautious when we crossed the famous Via Gregorio VII. Once I got home, I could replenish all the energy I had lavished on the parish soccer field at the dining room table. That, however, was just a brief intermission in my soccer-related activities. At two thirty in the afternoon, it was time for the most eagerly awaited event of the week: the Serie A soccer matches from all over the country, collectively reported on the radio.

The fact that I had eaten Sunday lunch at home meant that I hadn't gone to see the game at the Stadio Olimpico with my father. So the only option was to listen to the match on the radio. That meant one of two things. Either I could head back to the parish soccer field with my friends and listen to the play-by-play in their company (one or two transistor radios always seemed to be available for that), or I could stay at home and devote my full and undivided attention to the voice of the radio sports announcers. As the minutes of play ticked by, I always did my best to memorize the exact timbre of the voice of the sports journalist covering my team, S.S. Lazio. Every time one of the dozens of sports announcers covering soccer matches across Italy broke in to announce a goal, I could feel a stab of excitement as my heartbeat raced and I furiously tried to concentrate on whether or not that voice was coming from the field where Lazio was playing. The sports announcers often had remarkably similar voices, and it wasn't uncommon for me to punch the air in thrilling exultation as the announcer shouted, "Goal!," only to sink back to earth as I realized it was another team—not Lazio—that had scored.

Once the soccer games were over, in order to recover from the psychic and physical ordeal of up-to-the-minute radio coverage—and while the grown-ups sat around groaning or napping after stuffing themselves with *ragù*, *involtini*, and *pastarelle*—we kids hurried back to the soccer field to play away the rest of the afternoon, until the darkness of late evening if our parents would let us.

Afternoons playing soccer were hardly limited to Sundays. In fact, school or no school, whether it was 105 degrees in the shade or raining cats and dogs, every blessed day of the week we had to play right up to the last possible moment. In the winter, we developed echolocation skills worthy of so many little bats: we kept running up and down the field even when it was too dark to see. I remember playing one-on-one matches and being one of the last two kids left running around in the dark, when my parents would come down to the field to drag me home—I protesting vociferously, they furiously lecturing me about having called every hospital in Rome to look for me before thinking of the soccer field.

A terrible threat, however, loomed over our midweek soccer matches: the hour of catechism. Out of the sixty children busily chasing the soccer ball back and forth across the field, fifteen at a time were hustled off the field to attend the sixty-minute class in the parish church. The match was stopped a few minutes before the hour, and those who were going to be marched off to study left the field, weeping, moaning, throwing tantrums. The rest of us simply hardened our hearts and resumed play.

Luckily the parish soccer field was surrounded by a ring of overgrown hills covered with bushes and shrubs. Roughly fifteen minutes before the hour, those hills began to fill up with the tousled heads of youngsters hiding in the shrubbery, doing their best not to be hauled off to catechism. Still playing on the soccer field were those of us who, by some fluke of destiny, weren't required to attend the class taught by the parish priest.

Once the roundup was over, a few minutes after five p.m., the horde of hobbits emerged from the underbrush and the game resumed. We never wanted to stop playing.

When the game finally, inevitably came to an end, we returned home in a state of indescribable filth. The least exciting part of the routine began for all the midget soccer players in my neighborhood: wash time. I don't know how many kilograms of dirt a child can actually bring into a house after the kind of soccer matches we played, but I do know the dirt was everywhere: coating our arms, smeared on sweaty soccer jerseys, caked in the creases and wrinkles of our shorts. And even though I would have happily climbed into bed in that state—just to save time for everyone; after all, ten minutes into our game the next day, I'd immediately resume my state of filth—my mother would decline my labor-saving offer and send me off to the bathroom for a thorough bath.

I tried to negotiate with her to let me take a bath every other day instead of every blessed evening, but there was nothing doing. The thing that pained me most was that, because of my mother's stubbornness, I was excluded from a very special competition: the rainbow foot contest. That's right, because at the end of the seventies every kid in Rome wore the same kind of shoes: the formidable MECAPs, newfangled creations made of rubber and canvas, in a color somewhere between dark blue and green. They had one fundamental flaw: when they came in contact with a sweaty foot, the dye never failed to run. This not only stained your socks in a way that made them unusable in future, but they also stained the foot in an incredible spectrum of bizarre hues. These spontaneous artistic creations that appeared unbidden, printed into our feet, were vaguely psychedelic, hypnotic, and wonderful. Most importantly, they were a field for competition. We could sit there for hours admiring these found works of pop art that explored the entire range of blues and greens, masterpieces that could rightly have been acquired as part of the collection of contemporary art at MoMA. But back then, like so many geniuses, we were misunderstood. Only the most daring, or the luckiest—those, in other words, who managed to stay out of their mothers' clutches, either with superior negotiating skills or a particularly good excuse, and kept from washing their feet for two or three days in a row—could aspire to victory in the rainbow foot contest. For sure, after the Sunday soccer match, I didn't have a chance: not only were my feet washed, they were even disinfected with ethyl alcohol until they returned to their natural color.

After the evening bath, it was bedtime for us midget soccer players—at least during the week. But on Sunday evenings there was one last magical moment: the show *90° minuto*, or 90th Minute (a reference to the length of soccer games, ninety minutes). This was a sports broadcast that all Italy watched fanatically. The opening theme music was unmistakable, and any Italian would recognize it instantly, even if you woke them up in the middle of the night with it. The show reprised every goal scored that Sunday, and until we actually *saw* them on *90° minuto,* we had only been able to imagine them when we'd held our transistor radios to our ears. The cue that our beloved Sunday soccer special was about to begin any minute now would come from the closing theme music of the preceding program, *Attenti a quei due*, a show better known around the world by its original English name, *The Persuaders!* From the beginning of *90° minuto* until late Sunday night, when I was finally frog-marched off to sleep, I plunged into a rushing river of soccer television, summaries of epic games, replays, and commentary. As far as I was concerned, I could watch this stuff forever. And if that Sunday my beloved Lazio had won, then I dropped off into a golden slumber. If not, I would toss and turn before finally falling asleep, troubled by the idea that tomorrow, back at school, I'd have to resume the daily battle with my friends who were Roma fans. Like the eternal conflict between Good and Evil.

Of course, I was on the side of Good.

5

❧

Secret o' Life

7 hardly need to say it: as far back as I can remember, like many other Italian boys, I had decided, beyond the shadow of a doubt, that when I grew up I was going to be a soccer player. The question of talent—*maybe* that was something I lacked—was a side issue. The crucial point was this: it was all I did all day, every day, with my friends at the parish church, from midafternoon until sunset, and then I continued playing on my own at home. I couldn't imagine doing anything else when I grew up. When it got dark out and I finished playing at the parish church, I would return home and start dribbling again on the terrace—either convincing my father to play with me or else dribbling and kicking the ball against the wall by myself. I think it was an ongoing nightmare for my mother: from the filth that covered me from head to foot every

time I returned home, to the relentless hammering of the soccer ball against the outside wall of the living room, it must have been hard on her. Only the love of an Italian mamma could have made it possible to put up with this regime of torture. I think that if there was a child like me in my apartment building today, I'd pour a pot of boiling pasta water on his head from my balcony!

What with playing every day from morning till night, I felt sure I was becoming better and better, and at night, under the blankets, I dreamed of my long career as a soccer player, a crescendo of triumphs. I would play for one team and one team only, my beloved S.S. Lazio, until I was drafted for the Italian national team. Then I'd go on to win the World Cup final match with a decisive last-minute goal in the most hotly contested minutes of play in the history of soccer, and my roar of joy would ring out like a cross between Rocky Balboa in the boxing ring and Marco Tardelli in the 1982 final match against Germany. I would raise the World Cup over my head as I looked out over an ocean of streaming Italian tricolor flags—as I stepped, once and for all, into the halls of legend.

How many times I luxuriated in these golden daydreams . . . But each time, a little serpent of nightmare wriggled into my fantasy, hissing the inviting sound of my surname. What if, instead of scoring the winning goal, I made the Italian national team lose the World Cup with a decisive and devastating *own goal*? What banner headline would be screaming across the front page of the *Gazzetta dello Sport* the following day? I had no doubts: Spaghetti-Ball!

Now, it's true I had always played the inside forward position, so I was usually closer to the opposing net than our own. The likelihood was greater, therefore, of scoring a goal than an own goal, but unforeseen factors always lurked in the wrinkles of the game: a ricochet on a penalty shot, a chance deviation on a corner kick—you could never know. In short, Spaghetti-Ball was a constant danger. Of course, if this potential own goal were to be made by Carlo Bianchi or Mario Rossi, it would be an entirely different matter. No one would be able to think up any cutting puns on their names.

Yet it didn't keep me from dreaming. Or from rooting furiously for the team I loved above all others, S.S. Lazio.

I was born with Lazio in my heart. Or at least I think I was, because I can't remember the exact moment when I became a die-hard Lazio fan. So I've probably always been one. Certainly, the celebrations in 1974 when S.S. Lazio won the *scudetto*, Italy's national soccer championship, for the first time in the team's history invigorated my loyalty, but in all likelihood it was the steady stream of subliminal messages being broadcast by my father, a dyed-in-the-wool Lazio fan, while I was still in my mother's womb that turned me into the all-out *laziale* that I am and have been for as long as I can remember.

S.S. Lazio, Rome's first soccer team, was founded in 1900 in the heart of the city, at Piazza della Libertà, a magnificent "balcony" overlooking the Tiber. Even now, every year Lazio fans spend the evening of January 8 in Piazza della Libertà, waiting for midnight to celebrate the birthday of their one and only team. The team's colors— white and sky blue—were selected in honor of Greece, homeland of the Olympic Games. As for the club's badge and symbol, the founders weren't timid: an eagle with its wings spread, a proud emblem of the legions of ancient Rome.

How could a child resist the allure of such a story? And it all would have remained very poetic and sentimental, had an irreparable disaster not occurred twenty-seven years later. Four smaller city clubs merged to create a new team: A.S. Roma.

Roma fans proliferated like rabbits, and as I write this, there are probably seven times as many Roma fans in the city as there Lazio fans. That of course does nothing to undermine my love—and the love of my many friends who are also Lazio fans—for the white and sky blue jersey. Maybe there's also a kind of strength in *small* numbers. But Roma fans are hard to miss, especially considering the team colors: just look at the difference between the elegance of Lazio's white and sky blue and Roma's garish yellow and red—any fashion designer or couturier would have to agree with me!

In the late seventies, when I first began to follow soccer as a genuine fan, S.S. Lazio was unfortunately a team in serious trouble. In the years that followed, disasters of every kind were visited on poor Lazio. What's true in love is also true in soccer: the more you love, the worse it hurts. There was one bad year after another, culminating in the official downgrading of S.S. Lazio to Serie B as a punishment for an illegal betting ring linked to the club. It certainly wasn't the fans' fault, but the dishonor besmirched us as well as our team. I continued to show up for soccer at the parish field in my white and sky blue jersey, but clusters of kids wearing yellow and red jerseys seemed to grow constantly, and it was all too easy for them to ridicule a fan of S.S. Lazio, now struggling along in Serie B. Add to the mix the name Spaghetti . . .

It was hard to withstand the constant ribbing. And every time we tried to organize a mini crosstown derby among us kids, it was always three or four outnumbered Lazio fans playing against a far more numerous and enthusiastic group of eleven *romanisti*. Maybe that was why we *laziali* just kept getting better and better. It was the misfortunes of our miserable S.S. Lazio that taught us young fans how to lose, while our little yellow-and-red-jerseyed cousins hadn't yet really learned how to win.

It wasn't until the 1982–1983 championship season that S.S. Lazio climbed back up into Serie A; unfortunately, that was the same championship season in which A.S. Roma took the *scudetto*, which spoiled my first taste of joy as a Lazio fan.

In those years, from when I was nine till I turned thirteen, it was always my dream to go see a soccer match at the stadium. To turn that dream into reality on anything like a regular basis demanded suitable preparation. First of all, if I wanted even the slimmest likelihood of success, I'd have to start hammering at my father several weeks before the match in question. Once I had begged and pleaded him into compliance, the breathless countdown to Sunday began. We'd take a bus to Rome's Stadio Olimpico, to avoid problems with finding a parking place—even back then, a parking place was the holy grail in Rome. Since there was no numbered seating, we'd have a midmorning departure from our house, to ensure we'd have plenty of time to get to the stadium, buy our tickets at the box office, and select a good location on the curve behind the goal along with the rest of the fervent home-team supporters, usually standing up. And then . . . we waited, since the soccer match never began before two thirty p.m. The privileged ticket-holders for the bleachers, where seating was numbered, could afford to show up minutes before the first whistle marked the beginning of play. I didn't mind waiting in the crowded benches: I liked watching the excited, colorful crowds that surrounded me as I anticipated the magic of the match. Even though my father was a rabid fan, taking me to the stadium on a Sunday was probably more torture than pleasure for him. For one thing, it meant he had to give up Sunday lunch, a fundamental ritual for any self-respecting Italian family—and my family was certainly no exception. In fact, Sundays were when my mother and my grandmother together put on a display of dizzying culinary ability, and we spent hours lingering at the table, eating, talking, and drinking wine, enjoying the leisure time that is always in short supply during the week. Still, even if it meant skipping the Sunday banquet, it was always a special occasion when we went to the stadium, and having a *panino* for lunch was no big sacrifice. In fact, I can still remember clearly the flavor of the *panini al prosciutto* that we'd pack with us from home. The memory of that flavor is etched into my mind, and I'll always associate it with the intense excitement of those moments of pure fandom. I remember the first time I walked into the Stadio Olimpico. It was a sunny afternoon, and the sunshine made the grass seem even greener. Then I waited with bated breath for the teams to run out onto the field. Finally the match began. It was the first time I'd ever seen a game from the unaccustomed angle of the curve. Imagine my shock—silly, I know, but for me it was a surprise to discover it—that there was no play-by-play announcer, like on TV! Luckily, from years of watching Sunday evening sports roundups that showed all the goals of the day's matches, and thanks to my relentless study of the soccer player cards made by Panini, I had no particular difficulty identifying my favorite champions, even without the staticky voice of the announcer shouting their names every time one of them gained control of the ball.

In the eighties, I started going to see soccer games at the stadium with my friends, and often without my father. This was a hard time in Italy, and the Stadio Olimpico wasn't necessarily the safest of places. Italy's "years of lead," a period marked by terrorist attacks, civil unrest, and a fair amount of fighting in the streets, had only just come to an end, and grown-ups were cautious about letting kids wander the city unsupervised. Especially when there was a "derby" in the offing—what we called a crosstown game between S.S. Lazio and A.S. Roma.

In Rome, the derby and—much more important—the run-up to the derby passeth all human understanding: every fan, whether rooting for Lazio or Roma, has his own way of experiencing and awaiting the derby, his own superstitions and propitiatory rites. There are those who prepare for the derby dressed in the same clothes, year in year out, for decades. There are those who vanish for a week prior to the derby on a meditation retreat. There are those who whip themselves up into a furious frenzy, so that by the day before the game their eyes are bloodshot with snorting hatred for the other team and all its fans. And there are those who simply have nervous breakdowns.

I can't think of many other cities on earth where a sports event has so much importance to urban life. Every day in the pre-derby period, people in Rome wake up, wash their faces, make sure that there is only good news from their team's training camp, and then—only then—do they go to work. I've come to the conclusion that the true sports fan in Italy's capital does not so much love his team as he hates and wishes only the worst on the team from the other side of the Tiber.

And so, paradoxically, what I consider to have been my greatest triumph as a Lazio fan was the defeat of Roma by Liverpool in the finals of the Champions Cup on a penalty kick back in 1984. It was my revenge. Years before, Roma had ridiculed Lazio for their demotion to Serie B—for something that didn't even happen on the field. And now, thanks to that loss on a penalty kick, I fooled myself into thinking they would finally learn how to lose.

6

❧

Music

What rescued me from obsessing over the many obstacles of the Spaghetti name was, first and foremost, music.

The first song I ever sang was "Mamunia," by Paul McCartney & Wings, a beautiful acoustic track from their wonderful album *Band on the Run*. It was 1973; I was three years old and I still pronounced my own name "Cuca Petti." I was the first and only grandchild in my small family, and therefore the unrivaled sovereign of my parents' and grandparents' affections. Every time my grandparents saw me, it was a celebration.

My grandmother Liliana was born in Sardinia. She was very short. She was more or less the same height as E.T., and she had the same heart-melting gaze. As for my grandfather, he was my ticket to get a taste of the forbidden fruit of the vine. It was only on Sundays, when we had lunch at my grandparents' house, that I was allowed to have a taste of wine, nectar of the gods, which was rationed out sparingly, a few drops at a time, into my glass, while the adults watched attentively.

My two youngest uncles, Giorgio and Fabrizio, lived at home with my grandparents, their parents. They were the first to introduce me to their love of music. Since they were both in their early twenties in the mid-seventies, they listened to music all the time. I was born and raised in a family where there was always plenty of music; my father loved jazz, which played as background music in every room of the house every day. To be honest, though, however much I might have liked his jazz, I was much more excited by the music my uncles were listening to. I was absolutely fascinated by the long, orderly rows of LPs that filled their shelves: hundreds of album covers with thousands of colors, beautiful photographs, and words that were generally incomprehensible to me. One of the few words I thought I could understand—because I believed it was Italian, though I wasn't quite sure what it meant—was "Mamunia." I had claimed "Mamunia" as my own, and I sang it to the delight of my entire family, repeating this strange word endlessly, until the occasional friendly kick in the pants informed me it might be a good time to turn off the small—and possibly annoying—jukebox. But my uncles always loved my vocal stylings, so every chance they got they would put "Mamunia" back on the record player. When I heard the strains of my favorite song, whatever I might be doing, I broke off my game and came running to the stereo to resume my show as Luca, the Singing Midget. Then, one fine day, my uncles asked me, "Luca, do you feel like singing something a little more challenging? It's a song made up of just two words. It's called 'Ob-La-Di, Ob-La-Da'!"

And the infectiously cheerful notes of "Ob-La-Di, Ob-La-Da" issued from the two mysterious cubes that my uncles called "speakers," along with the beloved voice of my friend Paul McCartney. They had persuaded me that he was my "Uncle Paul," just an uncle a couple of times removed.

My uncles Giorgio and Fabrizio continually handled those records that I saw as magical objects. They placed them on the turntable with incredible delicacy, taking care not to leave fingerprints or scratches on the surface. Of course, I was forbidden so much as to touch that long row of gems, and since I was a good little boy, I never disobeyed. If for no other reason than the fact that I had my own musical toy: an orange *mangiadischi*—literally, a "record eater." Anyone who grew up in Italy in the fabled 1970s remembers these little record players, into which we'd slip 45s of sing-along fairy tales. It was a must-have for all kids of that era. I knew all the songs by heart, but even then, I have to admit, "Mamunia" and "Ob-La-Di, Ob-La-Da" meant a lot more to me. So imagine my ecstasy when, a few years later, I started singing—with no understanding of the English lyrics—"Yellow Submarine," or as we pronounced it, "Iello Sammarin," accompanied by my two uncles on their acoustic guitars.

I was about eight when I received a gift that changed my musical destiny once and for all: my first real album—in fact, my first real *double* album. A record with a red cover, with the faces of four smiling young men looking down from a balcony. For the very first time, with the help of grown-ups who guided me in the pronunciation of the words in English, I read the name of the group: The Beatles. My uncles immediately demanded that I learn not only this eminently musical word, but also the names of each of the young men looking down from the balcony. After a full day of torture and rehearsal, I succeeded: John Lennon, Paul McCartney, George Harrison, and Ringo Starr. And when they told me that Paul McCartney was the same friendly uncle who sang "Mamunia" and "Ob-La-Di, Ob-La-Da," I asked somewhat sheepishly if I could consider the other three old uncles as well. I was told I could, and from that day forward, to me those young men were just John, Paul, George, and Ringo.

My hands were too small to hold the record without touching the grooves, the way a grown-up could, so they taught me to hold the disk with two hands, fingers outstretched and the edge of the vinyl record braced against the flat of my palm.

Music

The first track was "Love Me Do," followed by "Please, Please Me" and "From Me to You." I listened to those three songs over and over again, without stopping. Every time the needle reached the end of "From Me to You," with my steady little forefinger I carefully lifted the tone-arm and put the needle back at the beginning of "Love Me Do." And so on, ad infinitum. I don't think I even heard the fourth track on the album until a month or so later. "From Me to You" was my first true musical shock: I could distinctly hear two voices singing the same words with two different melodies, one made up of high notes, the other of low notes. While the lower voice seemed normal enough to me, the higher one sounded a little loose, but still exceptionally beautiful. Listening to the other songs there were always these two merry voices—one high and sweet, one low and a little sharper—that would come together to make one dreamy sound. I didn't know what they were saying, but I was hypnotized. Marked for life.

A few years later, I invested all my savings in the first record I bought with my own money: *Double Fantasy* by John Lennon. Tragically, just a few weeks after the record came out, John was shot and killed outside his home in New York. I couldn't stop asking myself why anyone would have wanted to kill him, since he was only a singer who had written beautiful songs. Everyone around me was far too grief-stricken to give me an answer.

The record was incredible (aside from a few songs sung by a woman with a voice I had never heard before, at least not on my double album with the red cover). Even if the only tracks had been "Woman," "Starting Over," and "Watching the Wheels," I could have listened to it for hours.

"Woman" was at the top of the Italian hit parade; every Friday and Saturday around noon, the radio broadcast the top ten songs and the so-called *dischi caldi*—"hot records," or the songs that were in eleventh to twentieth place. To keep from missing the weekly hit parade live, I took a small transistor radio to school with me. I listened to it pressed up against my ear, turned down low, as I sat in the last row of desks to keep the teacher from hearing. Of course, in order to hear "Woman," which was hovering around first place, I had to put up with all the songs from twentieth place to second or third place, but it was worth it.

I was captivated by music, by *that* music, most of it American, and I wanted more. Every morning I walked out into the Roman sunshine with a few coins in my pocket that my parents had given me to buy a snack at school with. Often I decided to squirrel them away, without telling them. I finally skipped enough snacks to make my monthly musical purchase. There was a little record store directly across from my house, and I was the shop's youngest regular customer; the owner had gotten used to the curious, enthusiastic boy who walked into his record store as if it were wonderland, and I guess he must have liked me. Still, he was astonished every time I left the place with Paul McCartney's *Tug of War*, America's *Alibi*, or the Alan Parsons Project's *Eye in the Sky* under my arm. I would spend entire afternoons listening to music in that shop, and I did my best to follow the lyrics printed on the inside record sleeve.

The great turning point came when my uncles gave me free access to their enormous library of LPs, which by now was even bigger than before. I was now allowed to listen to their records even when they weren't there. It was the point of no return. It was the mid-eighties, and I suddenly had access to hundreds of records in their updated musical library. The challenge was now to catch up on no fewer than fifteen years of musical history that I had missed. I discovered Jackson Browne, the Eagles, and even more from my four British uncles. Studying and listening, I learned marvelous things. (For example, the song that I used to know and sing as "Lady B" was actually called "Let It Be.") I decided to proceed in an orderly manner: I would buy a copy of every one of those records for myself, artist by artist. I decided to start with the Eagles. Every Saturday evening, while most of my classmates were heading for the discotheque, I hopped on my moped and scoured the record shops of Rome, returning home with at least one trophy, though often used or with a torn-up album cover. Many stores would sell used records by unknown bands for mere pocket change. If they were American, I bought them. What were a few lire when my musical awakening was at stake? I was sucked into a maelstrom of desperation as I became seized with another sick obsession:

the yearning to play the guitar. There were just too many six-string stimuli vibrating in my brain. I was fascinated by the sight of fingers moving delicately across the various parts of that musical instrument, creating chords and harmonies, often by a bonfire on a warm night. I *had* to learn to play the guitar.

And there was one more thing, not of secondary interest: I had noticed that guys who knew how to play the guitar attracted special interest among the girls. Maybe if I got to be a really good guitar player, my last name would be overlooked.

So I asked my uncles to lend me their Eko, a beat-up old Italian-made guitar that wasn't worth much, but was perfect for a beginner. With a manual of chords and a pile of Xeroxed sheet music and chord charts, and, more important, by listening to music nonstop, I started to teach myself how to play the guitar. I can still remember the immense joy I felt when I achieved my first bar chord—I played that C major over and over again, all day long. I'm pretty sure that during the period my parents must have at least *thought* about doing away with me. They'd always encouraged me and my brother in all our artistic pursuits, but still, I have to imagine that an incessant, unending strumming would have sorely tested anyone's patience.

But I was slowly improving. By now, I even had a few songs in my repertory: a few of the easier Eagles songs, for instance, were the first ones I'd mastered. But it was when I moved on to the records of another American singer-songwriter that my musical life changed once and for all: James Taylor. It came as a surprise to me. I knew only two James Taylor songs, "Hard Times" and "Her Town Too," which I had included to fill up some extra room on a mix tape. It was the mid-1980s, and a new album was about to come out. More important, in September 1985 James was coming to Rome for a concert, his first ever in Italy, and my uncles were going to take me. I didn't have much time; it was already July. The simplest thing would be to tape his *Greatest Hits*, a 1976 white album that I had found at my uncles' house.

I listened to his album somewhat distractedly that summer, really enjoying his voice, but then Live Aid burst onto the scene and distracted me from my James Taylor studies. I fed on that two-day mega rock concert and came away from it completely stunned. It was a dream to see so many legends on one stage: from Queen to Crosby, Stills & Nash, from U2 to Phil Collins, Madonna, Neil Young, Sting, and Paul McCartney. They gave unforgettable, over-the-top, truly spectacular performances. I was swept up in that wave for the rest of the summer until school began in September, when I was supposed to be seeing James Taylor, whom I had almost forgotten about.

As the night of the show drew closer, I felt a stirring sense of excitement. This was my first real concert. An hour before it started, I was already standing, three rows from the front, with both my uncles, looking up at the Palaeur stage. Luckily I was already almost six feet tall—I'd be able to see everything without being shoved or blocked. I spent the hour before the concert looking around the Palaeur, one of the long-standing premiere concert auditoriums in Rome. It was slowly filling up, and the magnificent stage was full of instruments waiting to be picked up and played by the members of the James Taylor band.

And when the lights went out, I was ready for the fireworks, drumrolls, and artificial fog that would surely accompany the entrance onstage of none other than James Taylor, world-famous rock star. But he walked onstage alone, to thunderous applause and lit by a single dim spotlight, a smiling gentleman with a receding hairline, wearing a pair of jeans and an ordinary shirt and carrying his guitar. The applause stopped only when his long, slender fingers began sliding up and down the neck of his guitar, and a sound that had never been heard before filled the Palaeur as a completely silent audience listened raptly. It was "You Can Close Your Eyes," and when James Taylor began singing the words to that song, I felt as if I'd been hit in the face by a solid right uppercut. I was paralyzed. He had an incredibly magnetic presence, verging on the hypnotic. He was alone on the stage with his guitar, but it sounded like three guitarists playing at once. As he sang, he smiled at the audience and even looked individuals right in the eye. I'm pretty sure a couple of times he even looked me in the eye, probably wondering what a fifteen-year-old was doing sitting bug-eyed in the middle of an army of somewhat nostalgic forty-year-olds. He would finish one song, to the very restrained enthusiasm of his audience, and then he'd begin another that always seemed to be the concluding crescendo, even though we were still just at the beginning: "Wandering," "Carolina in My Mind," "Sweet Baby James." He seemed like a guy who was just playing the guitar for a group of friends, baring his soul. Even to a young Italian boy who didn't understand the words, the genuineness of his feeling was clear. He didn't need walls of fire or balls of flame; he didn't need to cut bats' throats onstage to catch anyone's attention. All he needed was his voice, his guitar, and the immense talent he infused into both, as if it were the simplest thing in the world. His band made its entrance onstage and the concert continued, with such masterpieces wafting out over the audience as "Your Smiling Face," "Steamroller," "You've Got a Friend," "Up on the Roof," plus a number of songs from his new album, *That's Why I'm Here*, before the show concluded with "That Lonesome Road," a solo vocal interpretation that just knocked me out.

I was stunned, and when I returned home that evening, I was annoyed, even a little angry, with my two uncles. How could they have failed to inform me earlier that besides John, Paul, George, and Ringo, I had one more older uncle, the best one of all: James?

Actually, it was just the beginning of a long love story. I've since had the privilege of meeting my favorite singer-songwriter repeatedly, and I can now claim without fear of contradiction that I am the official welcoming ambassador to James Taylor in Rome. The first time I met him was in May 1992. At the end of a James Taylor concert, I successfully persuaded a security guard to let me go in and say hello to him when he was done talking to the press. I just wanted to ask for an autograph, I told the guard. In reality, I had written and memorized a speech that was basically an adoring love letter. I pestered this security guard so relentlessly that, in the end, he gave in and ushered me into his august presence. I held my girlfriend Giuliana's hand, and when I saw James Taylor standing at the far end of the room, talking to a couple of reporters—like Moses on the shore of the Red Sea—my heart leaped into my mouth. I walked up to ask him for an autograph. At that crucial instant, I forgot the speech I had written and rewritten for years. My mouth flew open and out came a single idiotic word: "Congratulations!" I turned to slink off, but after taking two steps, I spun on my heel, threw my arms around his neck, kissed him on the cheek, and burst into tears like a three-year-old. He probably hadn't expected all that from a six-foot-tall twenty-year-old Roman, but I like to think he kind of dug it. When I hugged him, he hugged me back with the smile of an affectionate uncle, and he even patted me on the back a couple of times while the reporters all laughed and Giuliana rubbed her eyes in disbelief.

The second time was in 1997. James came to Rome to

do publicity for his new record, *Hourglass.* He wouldn't be doing any concerts, but he would be interviewed on a radio program, and of course I immediately found out which one. My brother and I jumped on my scooter and, armed with cameras, we zipped over to the radio station. And there was my idol, smiling serenely, walking out the front door of the broadcasting center. We got a few pictures of ourselves with him, and in place of my moronic "Congratulations!" of a few years earlier, I actually managed to stammer out something that—I hope—made sense.

The next time was 1999, and after that, 2002. That year James Taylor played in a very special place in Rome. He held a free concert in Piazza del Popolo. That was the one time I was unable to see him in person, because of the huge crowd and the unique location of the event. There was no place to stake out the entrance, no way of sneaking up on the performer.

I made up for that two years later, when James came back to Rome in May 2004 for a concert at the Cavea, the open-air arena of the Auditorium Parco della Musica. During the day, the Cavea is a public facility, where people are free to stroll and enjoy drinks or eat ice cream. It's only during the soundcheck before a concert that the Cavea is closed to the general public—that is, the general public outside the Cavea at the time of the soundcheck. Not Luca Spaghetti, who's already been inside for a good hour. The soundcheck is probably the best time to try to have a brief conversation with a performer without bothering him or her too much. There's never a crowd, and the performer isn't full of pre- or post-show adrenalin. And so, that afternoon I got the best photograph ever taken of Luca Spaghetti and James Taylor, sitting side by side and smiling in the arena.

I even left Italy to follow my idol, from Frankfurt to Brussels, but I would have gone to the ends of the earth to see him play. In 2008 I waited to see him in front of the Gran Teatro of Rome, standing in a biblical deluge for hours. He arrived in a small tour bus with his staff, and when I saw him I asked him if I could come in to have my picture taken with him. With his customary courtesy he agreed, and he even took my picture with his cell phone as I was running toward him, dripping wet from the rain, to tell him thanks one last time.

Another thing I've always admired about James is the sweetness and serenity with which, every time he sings a masterpiece written by others—say, "You've Got a Friend" or "Up on the Roof" or "How Sweet It Is"—he never fails to thank and pay tribute to the composers and lyricists. He's always done it, at every concert of his that I've attended. He could easily say nothing at all, but instead, with the magnanimity of the truly great musician, he always mentions the names of those to whom he is indebted.

So let me finish by saying that before James Taylor decides to report me to the police as a stalker, it's really just that I adore him. And that, if I wait devotedly for his return and do everything I can to see him every time he comes to my city, it's only because I want to express to him the warmest greetings and collective hug of welcome that Rome can extend to a particularly rewarding guest. The part that makes me happiest in all this is that I have succeeded in communicating this passion to all my friends, near and far. On the other hand, seeing how I've tortured them over the years with my fervent love for James Taylor, it's understandable that every time they hear his voice or someone mentions his name, they have no choice but to think of me . . .

7

◉

There We Are

To summarize, until I was around twenty, my life was made up of just two magical components: soccer and music. Admittedly, I thought about girls a lot, but when I was with my friends and I saw a soccer ball rolling across a field, there wasn't a supermodel alive who could distract me from the enchantment of that leather sphere.

Of course, there was school and studying, but luckily for me, a few hours of hard work seemed sufficient to bring home consistently high marks. So once I got my homework out of the way, duty made way for enjoyment. During Italian high school—*liceo*—I actually managed to wrestle my parents into signing a "contract." For every good mark I brought home, they'd pay a certain amount of money. There was a price list: in Italy, grades range from a low of 1 to a high mark of 10. If I got a 6, no money changed hands, because that meant merely passing. For a 5, I was still in the clear because, while not much of a grade, it was acceptable, and just missing the passing mark could happen to anyone. If the grades were in the range from 1 to 4, it was a disaster. I didn't have to pay a penalty, but a tongue-lashing awaited me when I got home. And from 7 to 10, the grade range that I longed for and dreamed of, I was actually paid the cash bonuses we'd agreed upon. It was a wonderful little mechanism, and I took full advantage of it. I diligently prepared for my various oral examinations, "volunteering" to be tested once I was well versed on a given topic. Accordingly, my personal LP fund for Saturday afternoons was brimming over with cash during my high school years.

Music—listening and playing—and soccer—watching and playing: that's how my days flew by.

Since I've always been a pretty generous kind of guy, I enjoyed sharing the joy that I got from music with others. I was a fanatic about making compilations—I thought a compilation was a much more personal gift that just an impersonal album, purchased ready-made. In those days, before MP3s, iPods, the Internet, and all that, getting hold of the songs was a challenge. Creating a compilation tape was a long and elaborate process. I gave them as gifts to friends, relatives, and—yes—girls. I hoped that certain romantic songs would help me to win some girl's heart. After all, I reasoned, when a girl was listening to "You Can Close Your Eyes," even if she didn't understand the words, she'd have a much easier time forgetting that the boy courting her was named Spaghetti!

But the greatest satisfactions in that period came from my guitar. Studying James Taylor's songs was an excellent way of learning to play (and to learn English). The first time you hear them, many of his songs may seem very simple, because of his melodic style and the sweetness of his voice. Actually, though, they're really complex—at least they were for a self-taught guitarist like me. But after I learned to play a substantial number of his songs in a reasonably competent manner, I noticed with great pleasure that I had no difficulty playing 80 percent of the songs by my other favorite recording artists. And so, on summer evenings, on the beaches of Anzio, just outside of Rome, where, like many Romans, my family vacationed every year, we would often organize evening sing-alongs around a bonfire. I remember a nice big gathering of guys and girls, bronzed and dusted with sand and salt from a long day of sea and sunshine. Often grown-ups joined in as well from the balconies and patios of the surrounding houses, enjoying the cool on-shore breeze after dinner. In those long-ago summers, it was almost a daily appointment: night after night we got together on the beach and sang together, with cold beers and passionate summer love affairs that lasted a few days at the most. It was a simple but intense way of having fun, and it brought people together and created friendships.

I didn't always play my favorite pieces, but hearing my

friends all singing to music I played was a deeply moving experience. There was nothing that compared to the feeling I got when someone would ask me to play a song by the Beatles or James Taylor, or when I sang one spontaneously, only to find that someone else in the group knew it too and was happy to sing along with me.

Like everyone else I knew, I was waiting for my true love to come along, and in my heart of hearts I hoped that the charm of my guitar stylings would simply make the girl who was destined to be mine fall into my arms. Unfortunately, everyone kept asking me to play the guitar, and so evening after evening I played and played, and meanwhile everyone else was breaking off into couples and moving down the beach. Where I come from we describe that kind of situation with the pithy and eloquent expression *reggere il moccolo*—literally, "holding a candle." But not the way it's meant in English—rather, it means just standing there holding a candle so others can do whatever it is they're doing. At least holding that candle did nothing to keep me from playing my guitar, from which I was then truly inseparable.

When it came to girls, I have to say that soccer wasn't proving to be very helpful. I was playing at a more serious level in that period, competing in official and amateur regional tournaments. I fervently hoped this would impress the girls, but I was brought face-to-face with a great and profound truth: women and soccer don't mix! Quite the contrary. I should have figured it out from the pop song that used to play constantly when I was a kid. "Oh why, oh why do you always leave me alone on Sunday, to go watch the soccer game at the stadium?" wailed the despondent, and slightly angry, Italian pop star Rita Pavone. Her cry came from the heart, and it perfectly summarized the protests of millions of neglected Italian women who spent their Sundays alone because their men were focused on watching twenty-two overgrown boys in shorts and jerseys chasing a ball across a field. But Italian men must have other aces up their sleeves, because once Sunday soccer was over, peace was restored. And no one's ever heard of a marriage that ended just because of one Sunday soccer match too many.

As for me, I discovered to my own chagrin that girls were really, truly, deeply indifferent to my noticeable improvements at dribbling, kicking, or defense. They seemed equally impervious to the fascinating details of what formation S.S. Lazio was likely to field that Sunday. So I can assure you that the girls weren't exactly dropping at my feet . . .

During my first years at the university, I finally managed to coax my father back to the Stadio Olimpico. A sizable group of fans and friends had grown up by now, and we always assembled on Sundays in the same location—on seats that were finally numbered. No more leaving early for the stadium, packing picnic lunches. Now we enjoyed a leisurely Sunday lunch, followed by a bracing espresso, and then we'd hop on the scooter and zoom off to root for Lazio all together.

I usually spent Saturday evenings at the beach in Anzio,

even during the winter, with a group of friends, a group that had survived the end of summer. It was on one of those occasions that I met Giuliana. She was a beautiful girl, with light brown hair, green eyes, and a droll, gamine personality. What struck me in particular the first time I met her, though, was how unaffected she was, with just a hint of shyness. It was months before we actually managed to speak. She lived in Anzio and—miracle of miracles—my last name didn't seem to worry her a bit. As we got to know each other better, we grew even more fond of each other. One year after the evening we first met, we officially became a couple. I would tell my friends that the first time I'd laid eyes on her was as she was emerging from the waves, tan and golden and sinuous like Ursula Andress in the presence of a surprised and slightly stunned Luca "James Bond" Spaghetti, or I'd say I saw her running light-footed down the beach, like Bo Derek in *10*. What I never told my friends was that, in reality, of course, we had first met at dinner, over a steaming plate of pasta. Or, most important of all, that I had fallen head over heels in love with her.

Part Two

A ROMAN IN THE STATES

8

Up on the Roof

$\mathcal{A}$ mong my many boyhood dreams the absolute top ambition was . . . to go to America. I had always yearned to go to the States, starting when I learned my first songs in English. Though I was completely in love with my city, the most beautiful city in the world, deep down that American music stirred in me a kind of longing for all these places and landscapes I had never seen. I would tell Giuliana how much I would have loved to drive from Stockbridge to Boston, like in "Sweet Baby James," or from New York to the Golden Gate, like in "Wandering." And finally, my dream was about to come true.

It was July 29, 1995. I had just gotten my university degree and I was ready to travel. My parents had given me a wonderful gift: the trip to America I'd always dreamed of, a coast-to-coast journey from New York to California and back. My friend Alessandro would come with me, and I was finally going to see with my own eyes all those places that American music and movies had made me fall in love with. I couldn't believe it: I was going to drive on the same roads as on *Starsky & Hutch* and *CHiPS*, and maybe I could borrow Magnum P.I.'s car for the time I was there, or else rent an economy model of Kitt from *Knight Rider* (known to us in Italy as *Supercar*). And on my car radio, I'd be able to listen to all American music all the time, and I would go sailing at high speed down the highway through the Arizona desert, singing "Take It to the Limit," my favorite Eagles song, at the top of my lungs. I'd be eating hamburgers and French fries, beer and Coca-Cola, and pancakes with maple syrup for breakfast. Most of all, best of all, I'd have a chance to meet James Taylor. That's right, because I had read somewhere that he lived in Manhattan, and I felt sure that once I was there, one way or another, I'd be able to track him down.

Alessandro and I would be staying with an American family, at Patrick McDevitt's house. Patrick McDevitt was Alessandro's pen pal, and he lived in New Jersey, just a few dozen miles from New York. I hadn't met him yet, but this Patrick McDevitt had already become one of my heroes.

But we'd totaled up the check without consulting the innkeeper, as we like to say in Rome—that is, we still had to inform our hero and pen pal that two young Italian men would soon be invading his home.

We made up our minds to just go ahead and place an

intercontinental phone call to the home of Signore and Signora McDevitt. Alessandro and I pooled our resources and managed to come up with the considerable sum of ten thousand lire to purchase a phone card. We found a phone booth far from our respective apartments, because if our parents had caught either of us on the family phone calling America—in the middle of the night because of the time difference and at some unknown but undoubtedly vastly expensive cost per minute—they might very well disown us on the spot. But most important, Alessandro and I had agreed, looking each other in the eye with frank admission, that considering the embarrassingly bad level of our spoken English, if there was a cringe-inducing phone call to be made, better to do it together, in the privacy of a phone booth, than in the presence of other human beings . . .

We were pretty worried. We might be able to get out a few words of English, but would we be able to understand what the other person was trying to say to us? We agreed that, if it came to it, we could always hang up and run away. With these courageous thoughts in mind, we made the call.

The thankless task would fall to Alessandro, of course, because Patrick was his friend. And we shuddered to imagine what would happen if I had called and said something along the lines of "Hello, I am calling from Italy and my name is Luca Spaghetti . . ." Patrick would have hung up on me immediately, assuming it was a crank call. So we screwed up our courage and decided to go through with it: we both stepped into the phone booth and, with our hearts more than with our fingers, punched in Patrick's phone number. I'll never forget Alessandro's expression— pop-eyed with astonishment and anxiety—when someone answered the phone on the far side of the world. Alessandro stood there speechless, catching his breath after gulping down his anxiety—it must have been something like gulping down a whole hard-boiled egg—and then broke into a stream of excited, convulsive, hopeful English.

I couldn't understand a word of what he was saying, so I can imagine what the Americans made of it; anyway, the glowing display on the phone showed that the credit available was plummeting at an incredible rate, like a time bomb in a movie. In just a few minutes our hard-earned ten thousand lire was gone in a puff of smoke, but Alessandro had done it: once we got to New York, Patrick would come to pick us up at the airport, and we could stay for a few days at his family's house in New Jersey.

Just a few days later, our plane landed at JFK Airport. All that stood between us and American soil was the terrifying immigration control. During the flight, even before landing, we had had to fill out the notorious green form that asked whether we were spies, had any infectious diseases, or were guilty of genocide; it immediately struck us that the best idea might be to answer no to all of the above. There was just one question we would have liked to answer yes to: "Are you bringing more than ten thousand dollars per person to the United States?" Unfortunately, the answer to that one was also no.

Despite everything—despite our rumpled, demented appearance, the result of the time difference, the jet lag, and the Finnair flight with a one-day layover in Helsinki—we were admitted into the United States of America. I couldn't believe it—my dream was finally coming true!

As we walked out into the concourse, we found Patrick waiting for us, all American and smiling, just as I'd imagined him. Unfortunately, his smile disappeared the minute he realized he would have not one but two Italian guests; five seconds later, it dawned on me that the ten thousand lire we'd spent on the phone card had been a complete waste, that Alessandro and Patrick hadn't really understood one another at all, and that absolutely no provisions had been made for me to stay at Patrick's house. Once we got past the initial shock, though, it turned out there was no problem. In fact, the welcome I received at Casa McDevitt remains one of my finest memories of my trip to the U.S.A. Even though we were exhausted from the jet lag and all we were dreaming of was a mattress to collapse on, Pat's mother had made dinner for us. When we walked into the dining room, I saw that there was nothing but a bowl of salad on the table. I relaxed. I told myself, *They're just going to give us some salad, and then we can go to sleep.* Immediately afterward, though, a familiar aroma wafted out of the kitchen, ringing alarm bells in my mind. From that moment on, it became clear to me. In Italy, salad is a side dish served with the *secondo*; in America, it's a prelude to dinner proper. And in fact, then I saw Pat's mother emerging from the kitchen with a huge bowl of spaghetti with tomato sauce! And after that, a delicious roast, and then dessert. And I thought I'd be eating only hamburgers and French fries in the U.S.A. . . .

After dinner, we retired to the living room, where I found myself with a guitar in my hands, playing songs for my new American friends, songs by my American heroes— James Taylor and Jackson Browne and Jim Croce. It was a magnificent evening. I would never have expected to find the same warmth I knew from the bonfires on the beach at Anzio thousands of miles away from home.

I was happily exhausted, but I couldn't think of sleeping: it would be just a few hours now until I set foot in New York! I've never felt such a strong and abiding excitement about going to see a city. I kept wondering if it would be just as I imagined it: big, magical, filled with music and color, modern and breakneck and frenetic.

When I first glimpsed the Manhattan skyline from the bus, I felt goose bumps all over my body. We were really about to enter the city that never sleeps! I got off the bus, as if we were being pulled by some immense invisible magnet, and before we knew it, we were in midtown, on Fifth Avenue. With no particular destination, Alessandro and I wandered, openmouthed, eyes wide open, hearts overbrimming with joy. I was speechless, though in those first few minutes I had come to at least one clear conclusion: in a city this size, I'd never be able to just run into James Taylor.

Manhattan was a thousand times more—more of everything than I ever could have dreamed. It was indescribable. We understood once and for all that this was a world apart when—as we walked along, stunned at the sheer size of everything we saw—Captain Kirk in person came walking across the street in our direction. Or perhaps I should say, someone *dressed* as the captain of the Starship *Enterprise*, undisturbed, was walking the streets of New York—a golden yellow long-sleeved shirt over a black mock turtleneck, and a pair of black trousers—to the complete indifference of passersby.

We tried to imagine the same thing happening in Rome. If Captain Kirk had descended the Spanish Steps in Rome, coming down from the Church of the Trinità dei Monti to Piazza di Spagna, there would have been a chorus of laughter, and surely some Roman gentleman or other would have ventured to ask him whether, considering the inevitable traffic problems of the Eternal City, he'd found a parking place for his starship, or whether he'd had to leave his keys with some sinister-looking self-appointed parking honcho.

But in New York, anything is possible, anything is normal, and anything can happen. Anything and its opposite.

It is not hard to see that I have always been an enthusiast

and an optimist. Even when things seem to be going badly, I can't seem to help seeing the glass as half full—and usually half full of a very nice Italian red. In fact, I'm often so damned optimistic that I don't even see the glass: I just see the red wine. (The truth is, every so often my friends suggest to me that I'm not really an optimist at all—maybe I'm just an alcoholic.) In any case, my enthusiasm always drives me to pursue my dreams with an unstoppable determination. And usually, so furiously do I chase after those dreams that eventually I manage to achieve them. Perhaps because of the energy I put into pursuing my objectives, though, I often have the sensation that I cannot fully enjoy the moment in which I see a dream come true. Perhaps, incurable Roman romantic that I am, what I'm really trying to do each time is to create a series of memories, stockpiling them for some future date but almost forgetting to enjoy them in the here and now. I've gazed transfixed at I don't know how many sunsets, entranced by their beauty but at the same time doing my best to capture the feeling of those moments in order to be able to remember them, someday in the future, exactly as they were.

And that first day in New York, stunned though I was by the all-encompassing excess of that incredible city, I still felt that I could hardly contain within my heart and soul the vastness of the dream I was finally achieving: the American dream of an Italian boy.

My legs were leading me through the Big Apple. Central Park left me breathless. It had first become a mythical place for me when, on a September evening in 1981, I watched the legendary Simon & Garfunkel concert on my TV at home in Rome. I spent the entire evening glued to the TV, and I recorded the whole event on my little tape recorder. I held it up to the speaker of our television set and sternly demanded that my entire family maintain the strictest silence. Luckily, the concert LP came out not long afterward, but I spent the first few weeks playing and replaying that hissing, staticky tape recording, learning the songs by heart. I loved "Mrs. Robinson," but the true eye-opener was my first encounter with "The Sounds of Silence," an authentic masterpiece. There are few other songs in which the voices of Simon and Garfunkel are so perfectly fused, few songs in which the music attains an equal level of perfection.

When we got to the World Trade Center, we slowly raised our eyes skyward, looking up at the Twin Towers, gazing openmouthed at those wonderful silvery structures that never seemed to come to an end. It was impossible to resist—we had to go up to the top immediately, to the rooftop of the world. It took us a full minute, aboard an elevator that looked like a spaceship, to be catapulted up to the roof of the north tower, well over thirteen hundred feet in the air. Up on the roof, the 360-degree panorama was truly unbelievable: as far as the eye could reach, the ocean was motionless, an immense expanse of blue cement. New York City looked like a giant hedgehog stretching northward, its quills luminescent with reflected sunlight, and the topknot of Central Park on its head. The Hudson and the East River looked like a couple of small creeks, and the Statue of Liberty, the Grand Lady of New York, was for once a Little Lady, still there, raising her light to give hope to those coming into port, looking down benevolently in her turn at the tiny wakes of foam that the watercraft left behind them as they crept slowly along, crisscrossing the seawater. There was an enormous sense of peace up there, so different from the frenzy that reigned in the streets and avenues that these two elegant colossuses surveyed from above.

Once we got back to earth, we decided to treat ourselves to an exquisite cultural experience: a visit to MoMA. We weren't exactly experts in the mystery known as contemporary art, and we were more accustomed to Italian museums, where, frequently, the newest painting is five centuries old. So we didn't really know what to expect. We enjoyed ourselves enormously, browsing among what struck us as a series of likable and whimsical oddities, especially the can of Campbell's tomato soup. But at a certain point during our trek through the museum, I stumbled on something that really left me speechless: a huge canvas hanging on the wall, brightly lit, and completely blank. The first thing that occurred to me was that it had been put there by clever thieves to replace the painting that was supposed to be there. If I hurried to alert the guards, they could lock all the exits and we'd still be in time to recover the stolen masterpiece. The next morning, my photograph would appear on the front page of the *New York Times*: "Luca Spaghetti, the Italian hero who thwarted the art theft of the century." As I got a little closer, though, I noticed a small metal label on the wall identifying the painting: *White on White*. White on white?! It was a famous painting by Malevich, and it was, in fact, completely white: it was hanging there, perfectly safe, and nobody had even dreamed of stealing it. When Alessandro came back to find me, I was still standing there, motionless, staring at *White on White* with a blank expression on my face, probably in the throes of an attack of Stendhal syndrome.

We took a moment to catch our breaths, and then we were off again, this time to visit the Dakota, the apartment building at the corner of Central Park West and West Seventy-second Street, featured in the movie *Rosemary's Baby*, but sadly famous as the site of the murder of John Lennon, on December 8, 1980. I still remembered the tragic footage from the news reports we saw in Italy, the wrought-iron gates at the front entrance of the Dakota, all the people gathering around in a sort of spontaneous vigil. I thought there might be a plaque, something put up in memory of John, but there was nothing. There was absolutely nothing outside the Dakota, but across the street, in Central Park, we found a commemoration of him: a place called Strawberry Fields, a large mosaic memorial featuring the single word IMAGINE.

Three years before that trip to New York, in 1992, I had visited the Beatles Story, the museum at the Albert

Dock in Liverpool. I can still remember how deeply moved I was when, thinking I'd seen the whole exhibit, I unexpectedly found myself in the last room: the walls were all white, and in the middle was a similarly white concert grand piano. On top of the piano was a pair of glasses with round lenses, like John's, while the notes of "Imagine" filled the heart of anyone who entered the room.

There were no words accompanying the music, but I thought of all the things John would have to say to the world today. I turned and walked out in silence.

Between all the dizzying events of our days in New York, we managed to find time to plan our coast-to-coast trip; we were scheduled to leave in three days. Before I'd left Italy, Giuliana had given me a copy of Jack Kerouac's *On the Road*. And as if my own brimming enthusiasm wasn't enough, reading that book was like trying to put out a fire with gasoline. I was hungry for miles, I wanted to devour them by the thousand, and I didn't care how. I was going to get to California, to San Francisco, by any means possible.

And the means that proved to be possible had a name: the Amtrak California Zephyr.

But before we left for the coast, one more unforgettable New York experience awaited us: a baseball game at Yankee Stadium with Pat and his dad, John.

We were excited, both because of all the new things we

were seeing and because—with all the things we'd learned in just a few days on American soil—we could finally teach something to this young nation: how to go to the stadium or, in this case, the ballpark! It didn't really matter that we knew nothing at all about the rules of baseball. We had grasped the general underlying meaning of the sport: you were supposed to hit the oncoming ball with a bat just as hard as you could and try to send it as far as you could. Once we were comfortably seated in Yankee Stadium, we knew that after years and years of experience at the Stadio Olimpico and the Roma-Lazio derby, that baseball game was going to be a walk in the park for us—a walk in the ballpark.

That night the Yankees were playing the Milwaukee Brewers. There was just one minor detail I needed to understand. "Which team are we rooting for?" I asked Pat.

It's a gift I have: I feel comfortable anywhere I go; even in a foreign country, among people I don't know, I feel at home the first day, a full citizen the third day, and before a week is out I'm ready to join the army.

This time I was moving faster than usual. I might not have been ready to join the army, but I was definitely ready to fight for the Yankees.

"Home team wears white," Pat replied.

Whenever something important happened, Alessandro and I joined in with the cheers of the Yankee fans, proudly rolling out our elegant hoard of shouts, jeers, and exclamations from the Stadio Olimpico, heaping Italian curses, oaths, and insults on the heads of the unfortunate Brewers. Poor guys. If it had just been a matter of the name of the team—they were Brewers after all—we would have been all for them. But as guests we had certain duties of allegiance!

Pat and his dad were highly amused by the lessons we were giving the relatively well-behaved American baseball fans in how to root with imagination and style, and we were proud to offer our small contribution. The fact that, in later years, Pat could never tell this story without laughing so hard that tears came to his eyes made me think that our enthusiasm might have been a little much even for a New York baseball stadium, but their love of the Yankees had infected us.

I had practically slipped into a sports fan's frenzied trance when I found myself in a completely unforeseen situation. Back then, I was a smoker, a heavy smoker—in the sense that every day a pack of Marlboro Reds, always and only Marlboro Reds, was my one certain traveling companion. Out in the open-air bleachers of Yankee Stadium on that warm evening, I had already smoked four or five cigarettes, and was just lighting another, when I sensed a giant shadow looming over me. The security guard, an enormous black man with a terribly serious expression on his face and a menacing voice, had already started to read me my rights. The first thing I thought was: *Shit, I must have filled something in wrong on that damned green form at the airport!* Then I realized I must have done something much worse, but there, inside the stadium—could it have been the cursing? No, it was much, much worse: the cigarette. I had smoked a cigarette in an outdoor stadium! Chastened and silent, I put my Marlboro back into the packet. While the security guard threatened that he'd bounce me out of the stadium if I so much as laid a finger on the corpus delicti, my unlit Marlboro Red, John did his best to explain politely that I came from a less civilized country, but the guard wasn't interested in hearing excuses. One more cigarette and Luca Spaghetti would have to use a telescope to get a glimpse of Yankee Stadium.

The game went on, and as I looked around I realized that everyone was smoking, including John, but they were covering their cigarettes with the palms of their hands, inhaling and exhaling in the most unobtrusive way possible. While I had been the only idiot smoking my cigarette as if it were the most natural thing in the world—even blowing smoke rings. I tried to imagine what would have become of that poor security guard if he had tried to get someone to put out their cigarette during the derby in Rome. Even if he was Steven Seagal, his ashes would probably be scattered on the surface of the Tiber in less than half an hour.

But it was okay. I'd learned an important lesson about how a smoker has to behave in the United States. Moreover, the Yankees won the game, and ever since then, they have been my baseball team: *Go Yankees!*

9

Riding on a Railroad

*E*arly the next morning, with backpacks on our backs, we were ready to set out on the great journey. After a few long back-to-back train rides, we made it from New Jersey to Chicago, where we would catch the Amtrak California Zephyr. We boarded our new friend, our new home, and settled in for the next . . . four days! It would be a challenge, no question, but we both like a challenge. There were just two small problems. The first one—and it wasn't that small, come to think of it—was how we were going to get enough to eat and drink for four days. The second problem, and this one was mine alone, was spelled out in a single, terrifying question: When would I be able to smoke my next Marlboro?

We decided we'd start by reconnoitering the train, scouting to ensure a minimum level of subsistence. The

Zephyr presented us with two immediate options: the first, and most attractive, was the diner car, but only passengers whose wallets were a little fatter than ours could afford to eat there; the second option was a sort of bar, serving pizza, soft drinks, and snacks of all kinds. At least we wouldn't starve.

It soon dawned on me, however, that, for a confirmed smoker like myself, I had signed on for a particularly absurd trip from hell. The train's loudspeaker was just announcing the name of the next station, with the proviso that it would be a "smoking stop." *What?!* I rushed back to our seats to get my pack of smokes, and when the doors slid open I was out on the platform immediately, Marlboro in my mouth, ready to take full advantage of this "smoking stop." Out on the platform, I walked over to an elderly black gentleman who was a member of the Amtrak crew. He had the amiable, reassuring features of Morgan Freeman, and was probably his same age. What mattered most to me was that he seemed to be facing the same challenge as I was, because he was a smoker, too. When he confirmed my worst fears, I felt like I'd been sentenced to death: as I suspected, not all station stops were smoking stops. Only when the loudspeaker specifically announced it could you get out and smoke. I was going to lose my mind! Luckily for me, though, I immediately made friends with Morgan Freeman—who was actually named Luis and was Brazilian. He would be traveling with us on the Zephyr nearly all the way to the Pacific coast, and he knew in advance at exactly which stops I would be able to step onto the platform and suck down a few unhealthy gulps of tobacco smoke.

Now it was time to go get something to eat, so Alessandro and I went off to sample the culinary delights available from the train's back pantry. The answer was concise and alarming: pizza and beer. That's it. For four days! There was a further distinction open to us, though. We could choose between the normal round pizza or a "pepperoni" pizza. To the Italian ear, at first, this was less than reassuring. Our *peperoni* are red-hot chili peppers, but when we discovered that in America pepperoni is a kind of salami, we knew what we'd be ordering. Pepperoni pizza and a refreshing cold Bud. That first meal was delicious and filling, if not exactly nutritious. Unfortunately, it began to get old pretty quickly—pepperoni pizza and Bud for four days. I don't have to tell you that, for the rest of my life, I'll never forget the taste of Amtrak pepperoni pizza.

Having placated our hunger as best we could, we decided to venture out on a brief exploration of our train. In our wanderings, we stumbled upon a wonderful, magical car—it was almost completely transparent. It seemed to have been designed expressly to give passengers a spectacular vista of the surrounding landscape, day or night. We were overjoyed, and we immediately began to imagine what an incredible spectacle would meet our eyes when we got to canyon country.

The miles and rails slid away rapidly beneath us, and by the end of the first full day we'd become acquainted with more or less everyone on the train, from crew to passengers. One big happy family traveling westward together.

And then there was the Steve factor.

Steve was a boy, about twelve years old, with dirty blond hair with reddish highlights, light complexion, and a dusting of freckles. He was the youngest in a group of four or five kids traveling together, probably accompanied by some grown-up in another car. He was certainly the most curious of the group. Or at least the most curious about me and Alessandro—two slightly out-of-place young men speaking Italian. He started buzzing around us, asking a series of increasingly persistent questions about who we were, where we came from, where we were going. He wasn't obnoxious, really, but whenever we tried to kick back or get a nap, his head of slightly reddish hair would pop out of nowhere, always ready to ask us questions that sometimes veered into the intrusive.

By the second day, we were sick of him. We took refuge in the transparent car, feigning a sudden overwhelming interest in the landscape, even if we happened to be going through a tunnel at the time. That evening, though, the unforeseen occurred. Alessandro and I had pulled out a deck of Neapolitan playing cards and we were playing a feverishly competitive round of *scopa*, a classic Italian card game. I'm not really much of a card player, but when you're killing time with friends, it can be an ideal activity. And while *scopa* has its rules, it's actually the easiest and most

relaxing card game there is. You only need to know how
to count to ten!

We were in the middle of a game, with two ice-cold
Buds on the table, when the much feared head of tousled
reddish hair popped up next to us.

We agreed to let him watch, and—point by point, hand
after hand—Steve never missed an opportunity to ask us
about the exact reason for each individual play or maneu-
ver. We answered him absentmindedly, doing our best to
focus on our game but especially hoping he'd get tired and
go back to his parents.

We had hoped in vain. Ten minutes later, instead of suc-
cumbing to boredom, the young American announced that
he'd learned the rules of the card game and, to our horror,
asked if he could join in. My hand gripped the neck of my
Bud in frustration, but I soon relaxed and suggested a fair
deal with the little pain in the neck. He could play cards
with us, but once he'd lost a certain number of games, he
had to vanish from our sight for the entire following day.
Steve found our conditions acceptable.

My eyes locked with Alessandro's, and the evil grins of
a couple of jaded cardsharps slowly spread across our faces.
Alessandro gave me the honor and pleasure of destroying
the little red-haired pest, and he sauntered off to take a
stroll. Pretending to make a gentlemanly gesture, which I
felt I could easily afford, confident of victory as I was, I
allowed Steve to be dealer. He dealt three cards to me,

three to himself, and four to the table, clearly showing that he had learned the basics of Italian *scopa*—this in spite of our explanations in fractured English, which had probably been more confusing than helpful.

Even during the first game, Steve gave signs of being less helpless than we'd taken him for. And thanks to a couple of strokes of good luck, he actually beat me. Beginner's luck, I thought to myself. But when the next two games followed more or less the same pattern, I started to get a little worried. If Steve kept beating me, we'd have to put up with the kid all the way to San Francisco. How was I going to explain this to Alessandro? Not to mention, my pride wouldn't let me be beaten by a rank beginner without winning so much as a single game! So, I have to confess, dear reader, I started taking furtive glances at his cards.

It didn't do a bit of good. Even though I was cannily eyeing every single hand of cards Steve held, he still beat me!

Luckily, just then Alessandro, who was a much more experienced card player, returned from his stroll. We were safe now: Alessandro would trounce him. The twelve-year-old agreed calmly to take on my friend, and I sat back to enjoy the massacre that would now ensue from a comfortable vantage point. Leaning back just behind the little punk's shoulder, so I could read his cards in case the need happened to arise . . .

Now Alessandro, brimming with confidence, began playing where I had left off. Different player, same results:

the damned kid won every hand! Even cheating for all we were worth, we couldn't win a single game against him! We were at our wits' end. We had to surrender to the inevitable: for the next two days, we'd have young Steve stuck to us like a tick.

One doubt remained, however. We'd both had the impression that, as he played, Steve was doing his best to memorize the cards as they were dealt. I asked him cautiously if by any chance that was the case, and he nodded. More important, he told us something that cushioned our sense of complete failure: he was a child superprodigy, a pint-sized genius with ridiculously above-average intelligence, and that he was traveling to Denver to attend a special school for the gifted. In practical terms, he had more or less the IQ of me, Alessandro, and a few of our smarter friends, all put together.

Our spirits rose, for two reasons: first, we suddenly felt less like hopeless idiots, and second . . . Steve was getting off the train in Denver!

Still, we couldn't get a wink of sleep that night. There was just one question that kept tormenting us: Of all the trains in all the fifty states in America, why did we have to get on the one with a goddamned twelve-year-old boy genius, ready to humiliate us with his superiority at an Italian card game he'd never played in his life, after systematically mauling our nervous systems for two whole days?!

.   .   .

The train rocked us westward through Illinois, Iowa, and Nebraska, stopping at such historic towns and cities as Princeton, Galesburg, Burlington, and Omaha. We looked out the windows as we crossed the majestic Mississippi River and then the Missouri River. Finally the train pulled into Denver, Colorado. Here we moved to the transparent observation car to enjoy the amazing spectacle of the canyons, which would begin just a little farther west. We were beside ourselves with excitement. Penniless, overjoyed, our tummies full of pepperoni pizza, we were ready to abandon ourselves to an experience that money couldn't buy: thrills and high hopes.

And the gift that nature gave us next was unique and unforgettable: a succession of narrow, winding gorges through which only a train called Zephyr could possibly have wended its way. There were no roads in sight, only the rails that guided the train slowly but inexorably through fissures whose names alone were sufficient to bring us to the verge of tears: Coal Creek Canyon, South Boulder Canyon, Fraser Canyon, Byers Canyon, Gore Canyon, Red Canyon, and Glenwood Canyon. Canyonlands National Park. Every canyon had a story of its own, a color, a scent.

The most magnificent gift that Canyonlands had to offer was the sunset. It took our breath away. My eyes had never glimpsed such a stunning procession of beauty in such a short time. It was almost more than I could bear.

That night we rumbled on from Colorado to Utah, and as luck would have it, the next morning I was awake around five a.m. My eyes, still filled with sleepdust, were dazzled by a strong, clear pink light, powerful, all-encompassing, but at the same time incredibly gentle and sweet. I was alone and stunned in the observation car, with a dawn all around me that stretched and nestled onto the placid waters of the lake outside.

I didn't know what the name of that lake was, but in a sense I didn't really care. All that mattered to me was that pink hue. The almost unnatural pink generated by the light of a dawn that—like every morning since the beginning of time—was reflected in the waters of the lake. And that morning it had chosen to reveal itself to me, and me alone, as if bestowing a personal gift.

Suddenly I felt a presence by my side. It was Luis.

"You like the show?" he asked in a fatherly tone of voice.

When I saw it was him, I felt a moment of embarrassment. He'd caught me in a moment of personal emotion over a pink lake at dawn. But I was also glad to have a witness: it meant that what I was seeing through the window of the observation car was real, not a hallucination or a dream.

"Luis, I'm speechless. I know that we're not far from Salt Lake City. Is this *the* lake?"

"Do you really want to know?"

"Yes. Or maybe no. Maybe putting a name on this marvel is too much. Maybe my memory of it will be enough."

"Good answer, kid. You're a good young man. Take

this light, carry it in your heart, remember it in your times of difficulty."

"Thanks, Luis. I'll do that. But why do you have a backpack on?" I asked him.

"I'm saying good-bye to my Zephyr. I'm getting too old to take the long trips. I have to rest for a while. But then I'll start over. New journeys, new faces, new stories, the same old canyons and lakes, but with a never-ending array of colors. I'm getting off in a couple of minutes. This is a smoking stop. You want to smoke one last Marlboro together?"

"Of course, Luis. I'd love to."

That Marlboro at six in the morning was drilling a hole in my chest. For the first time, my Marlboro didn't taste like a cigarette. I was standing on the platform of a train station somewhere near Salt Lake City, in the magnificent pink morning light, with a friend I'd met only a few days earlier. It was one of the most deeply moving moments of my entire life. And at that moment, I understood what I'd been trying to conceal from myself when I first felt his hand on my shoulder in the observation car. That I'd never see Luis again. That Marlboro tasted a lot like life, and that wise old man was saying good-bye to me, with a smile veiled with sadness. He wished me all the best and gave one last hug to the young Italian man who was about to burst into tears. Then he walked off into the pink sunrise of a Utah morning.

I went back to my seat, doing my best to conceal my sadness. Alessandro was awake.

"Alessandro, you can't imagine what I saw in the past hour!"

"I saw it all. I heard you leave, I looked out the window, and I haven't moved since then. You went to the observation car, didn't you? I can't imagine what you saw from up there, but I think I can guess. I've never seen a pink dawn like that in my life. What lake was that?"

With a smile and a newfound wisdom, I replied:

"Do you really want to know?"

10

Wandering

$\mathcal{O}$ur last day aboard the Zephyr was dawning. We were already savoring our final destination: San Francisco. Instead, however, with a seven-hour delay, we were rudely dumped onto the platform of a station marked OAKLAND.

To get to our fabled destination, we had to take a bus. The trip up to and over the Bay Bridge was a marvelous experience, and our first encounter with San Francisco by night was absolutely unforgettable. We had already been seduced by this new and equally fantastic American city— seduced and abandoned, since we'd found ourselves, after a four-day train trip, seven hours behind schedule, with nothing but a pepperoni pizza in our bellies, at two in the morning at the foot of the Bay Bridge like a couple of forlorn jerks, backpacks on our backs, without the foggiest idea of where we would be spending the night.

We wound up spending that night, exhausted but excited, on a bench on the Embarcadero, and still today the photo that immortalizes that night on a bench is one of my most precious mementos. The next morning, a long day awaited us. That afternoon, Corrado, the third pioneer in our trio, would be coming in on a plane scheduled to land at San Francisco International Airport. We were supposed to pick him up at the airport, so we rented a car, a fantastic candy green Nissan Altima. Inside was a genuine treasure: a car radio preset to every country music station for miles around! While Alessandro drove, I couldn't stop punching in stations and singing along at the top of my lungs to every song that came on—until my ears picked up the opening notes of "Take It to the Limit." God, I loved that song. It wasn't one of the first Eagles songs that I loved, but I can still remember the struck-by-lightning feeling when I happened to hear it once by chance—it was buried along with lots of other songs in one of the band's double CDs—while I was studying for a final exam in economics. When I heard all the instruments strike up the opening chord in unison and Randy Meisner's yearning voice began singing, extraordinary and sweet, I felt a shiver go through my entire body.

That day I decided that "Take It to the Limit" was my favorite song by the Eagles, bar none. Who could ever have imagined that just a few years later, driving on an American highway, I'd have heard it by chance while spinning the radio tuner knob . . .

Wandering

"So put me on a highway, and show me a sign, and take it to the limit, one more time . . ."

With Corrado in tow, the following day we set out to explore the beautiful city of San Francisco, with its cable cars, its stunning panoramic views, Chinatown—almost a city unto itself—the phenomenal bay, Alcatraz, and the Golden Gate. That wonderful, infinite orange bridge that I'd been dreaming of for years reminded me of another masterpiece by James Taylor: *"I've been wandering early and late, from New York City to the Golden Gate, and it don't look like I'll ever stop my wandering."*

It didn't look like we'd ever stop our wandering, either. The next day we set out for Yosemite, and from there, after driving for a few hours, we started our descent along the West Coast.

Driving in the United States isn't like driving in Italy, at least not on the highways of California. There are times when it's like watching a movie projected on your windshield. The vistas are so stunningly beautiful, and the landscapes stretch out as far as the eye can see. It's quite a difference from Italian highways, where the most you can hope to see is a panorama stretching out a hundred feet or so, before a tunnel, an arid expanse of rocks, or the usual road work intervenes to spoil the view and the nerves of everyone in the car.

The first stop along the coast was Monterey, after which we headed down the most beautiful part of the California coast, along Highway 1: the Big Sur area. This region, so

beloved by Kerouac, with the Santa Lucia Mountains looming high above the breaking waves, is absolutely spectacular. Then we pulled into the more heavily touristed Santa
Barbara, where the pleasures that awaited us were perhaps
earthier and less poetic but still quite noteworthy. We found
ourselves in a restaurant with a funny logo, an owl with two
eyes wide open, forming the two letters *O* of the name of
the place: Hooters. We had never heard the name of this
particular fast-food chain. We thought we'd tried them all,
from Mr. McDonald to Miss Wendy to Colonel Sanders of
Kentucky Fried Chicken. No, Signore Hooters was a new
entry as far as we were concerned. We took a quick look
inside and remained somewhat nonplussed by what we
saw—agreeably nonplussed, let it be said. There was
a crowd of young women in uniform and on roller skates
serving the happy customers. That wasn't all: the outfits of
the young waitresses, all in their early twenties, consisted
of nothing more than a skimpy white tank top, two sizes
too small and with a neckline cut so low that it seemed
wrong to call it a neckline, and a pair of super-short orange
shorts that left little indeed to the imagination. And that
wasn't all. All of the waitresses seemed to have one thing in
common—or perhaps I should say two things in common:
immense, savage rotundities were swelling and pressing to
explode from their necklines, so low that perhaps I should
refer to them as waistlines. And their skimpy tank tops were
doing very little to contain these amazing round phenom-
ena. The bra size of the least pneumatic of the girls was at

least the size of Dolly Parton's. In short, a panorama that could make Hugh Hefner himself go white as a sheet.

In two minutes, Signore Hooters was already another of our all-American heroes!

The following morning, we set out for our first swim in the ocean—not just any ocean, but the Pacific Ocean. It was quite a daunting undertaking for three young men accustomed to the placid, tepid waters of the Mediterranean Sea. I had barely dipped my big toe into the blue Pacific when I realized that there was no way I was getting into that water. The temperature was subarctic, and even ten liters of good Italian *vin brulé* would hardly suffice to warm my blood and restore my circulation if I took a dip in those icy waves. Corrado was braver than me. He was in the water for a total of two-tenths of a second, but he did in fact go in. It was a full twenty minutes, however, before his body got back the color of a living human being.

We wandered around the city until the middle of the afternoon, then climbed back in the car to head south to Los Angeles. On the radio "Ventura Highway" was playing, my favorite song by America, and when I noticed a sign reading VENTURA, I could hardly believe my eyes. We were listening to "Ventura Highway" on the Ventura Highway!

Los Angeles was an immense metropolis, and we weren't crazy about it. It was so big you never knew where you were. But how could we miss going to Beverly Hills and taking a look at the front gates of billionaires' and movie stars' mansions? Or taking a walk along the Hollywood Walk of Fame and strolling nonchalantly over the names of famous movie stars?

Best of all, a short tour of Rodeo Drive: that was the road where Julia Roberts, one of our personal goddesses, went shopping in *Pretty Woman*. I would give anything to see her smile and her unaffected beauty in person—what would I say if I happened to run into her? Would that ever happen in my lifetime? Probably not, but it doesn't hurt to dream . . .

I emerged from the dream when I noticed, not far away on Sunset Boulevard, a Tower Records, my favorite record store. Whenever I see that logo, my mouth starts to water. I had to go in, no matter what city I was in, to find all the records I'd never be able to find in Rome.

After leaving LA, we headed south toward our final destination on the Pacific coast, San Diego; a couple of hours' drive down the San Diego Freeway would get us there. San Diego was a magnificent city, with a hot, dry climate and colors and scents that reminded you Mexico was just a stone's throw away. Endless beaches with piers extending out into the ocean, stretches of breathtaking coastline reminiscent of Big Sur, with mansions and houses perched above the waves—like at La Jolla, living up to its name as "the Jewel"—and a sense of freedom and peace that made me fall in love with the place on the spot. After the requisite stop at SeaWorld we took the San Diego trolley from downtown to Tijuana, the "Door to Mexico."

Wandering

We had expected a village with little white adobe houses like those we had seen in the Speedy Gonzales cartoons. We stood speechless after crossing the border on foot. Where we'd expected a village, we saw a vast metropolis. We walked onto the Avenida Revolución, a street the size of New York's Fifth Avenue. We soon learned that you could find whatever you wanted—cheap—in Tijuana: tequila, cigarettes, marijuana, sex, food, drugs, you name it. We settled for round after round of margaritas and wonderful fajitas. With a few cartons of Marlboros tucked under our arms, we wandered back over the border to San Diego.

The next day, as I was strolling toward the Gaslamp Quarter, my eyes almost bulged out of my head: at the corner of Fifth and F streets, I saw a sign reading CROCE'S. It was Jim Croce's restaurant, currently run by his widow, Ingrid. The great man had died in 1973, and I never would have dreamed I'd find a restaurant dedicated to his memory here, in San Diego.

It was just incredible. Anywhere I set foot in the United States seemed to give me a musical gift; it was as if I were following a path marked out by the notes of the songs I loved best.

The next day, after all the walking and exhausting touring, it really was time to enjoy the beach—sunshine, hot sand, cold waves, and nothing else. We chose Mission Beach and Ocean Beach. At the end of the day, looking out at a breathtaking sunset over the Crystal Pier and the Pacific Ocean, we really had no choice but to take the wise advice of another American hero of ours, Forrest Gump: *Since we'd gone this far, we might as well turn around, just keep on going!*

It was time to start our coast-to-coast trip back to New York.

11

Highway Song

So we hopped on our Greyhound and headed for Las Vegas. Along the road, the bus made a rest stop, and as I got out I felt the most incomprehensible blast of heat I'd ever experienced in my life. For the first time, I knew what the desert really was.

Once we got to Vegas, we certainly weren't about to miss our opportunity to tour the casinos. My lucky numbers were 28 and 11, 11 and 28. I was ready to make a killing and leave Las Vegas a wealthy man. I was going to make a sound investment in the roulette wheels of Nevada: fifty bucks. More than that, I couldn't afford. And so, having performed all the necessary rituals to ward off bad luck and propitiate the gods of fortune, and encouraging one another in turn, we three operators from Ocean's Eleven walked out onto the Vegas Strip ready and eager to choose the unfortunate casino where we would doubtless break the bank. Fate selected the Excalibur.

We walked in with the swagger and determination of born winners, and sat down at the roulette table. I couldn't think of anything but my lucky numbers—28 and 11, 11 and 28—and so I laid down my first stack of chips on those numbers. No luck—neither number was a winner. On the other hand, both Corrado and Alessandro came up winners. Winning, however, exposed their extreme ignorance about roulette, and they both lunged to grab their winnings. Neither seemed aware that the croupier was responsible for distributing the winnings. With a look of disgust on his face, the croupier clearly would have happily hit them over the head with his stick.

In return, I'd have happily punched him in the nose, as he kept singing out "Place your bets" but never seemed to hit a 28 or an 11. Ten minutes later, my fifty greenbacks had vanished into the thin desert air. To make things even worse, in fact, they'd been won by Alessandro and Corrado, who happily continued to place one successful bet after another. Crushed, I abandoned my friends at the roulette table and went to phone Giuliana:

"Darling, I've lost all my money! But Alessandro and Corrado are winning like the sons of bitches they are!"

I barely had time to finish the phone call when I saw Alessandro's silhouette in the distance as he came running toward me: "I lost all my money! But Corrado is winning like the son of a bitch he is!"

It was self-evident: fortune was blind, but disaster could see us perfectly. We consoled ourselves with the thought that we were certainly lucky in love. At that point, we decided that Corrado would take revenge on our behalf and went back in to cheer him on. And since we Romans always *exaggerate*—in our actions, in our obsessions, in our mannerisms—we rooted the way we had at Yankee Stadium. Corrado wound up winning over a hundred dollars. At least he had broken the bank at the Excalibur!

The next day was devoted to the Grand Canyon. The road leading there proved to be beautiful: desert, scrub, the Hoover Dam, uphill and downhill in blistering hot sunlight. Once we were near the park, though, it didn't strike us that we were any closer to our destination—we hadn't seen any ridgelines, mountains, or deep valleys that might suggest there was a canyon in the vicinity. Because if there's a canyon, you notice it. On our right, running parallel to the road into the park, there was a thick wall of bushes. We noticed a succession of familiar forms sticking out of the bushes: the rear ends of one human being after another! This series of people, for some reason that eluded us, had chosen to jam their heads into the bushes.

Overwhelmed by our curiosity, we parked the car and pushed our heads through the bushes. What I saw on the other side was indescribable: a red-rock canyon plunging hundreds of yards down from a perfectly flat horizon into the distant depths, where a tiny Colorado River meandered along.

It didn't look real. It looked like a spectacular painting done by the hand of God. It was immense, with a varied gradation of hues—red, yellow, orange, pink. The surface was a perfectly flat line, from which sheer walls descended straight down, eroded by millions of years of flow of the waters of the Colorado River. It was a deeply shocking experience—I felt as if I'd lost all sense of depth and proportion.

We stayed for as long as the daylight would permit us. When it was completely dark, around nine at night, we got back in the car to head back to Las Vegas. We left with a deep sense of gratitude and respect for the gift our new friend, the Grand Canyon, had given us.

It was about eleven p.m. and I'd been driving for a couple of hours while my two friends slept. In the distance, I saw a strange glow that you might say resembled the northern lights or E.T.'s spaceship. As we got closer to Las Vegas the glow increased, but it was only when we drove over the top of the last hill before entering the city that we understood what that glow was: it was Las Vegas itself! It looked as if a volcano had erupted and its glowing lava had covered the city in a giant luminous blanket. Once again, we were struck dumb—this time, in the presence of an incredible man-made creation: a sea of light in the middle of the desert.

Our trip eastward would continue the following day. Given the experience we had already accumulated and the fact that we'd become accustomed to traveling hundreds of miles every day without effort, we opted for the cheapest but also the least comfortable option: three days by Greyhound, from Las Vegas to New Orleans.

Because the bus made plenty of stops, we managed to get a glimpse—a short one, admittedly—of many American cities, from Phoenix to Tucson (which cities made me think of Dan Fogelberg, another favorite of mine) and then El Paso, San Antonio (I got out of the bus whistling Dan Seals's "San Antone"), and finally Houston. And then we reached our destination: New Orleans. We went for a walk and stumbled onto a place called the Cat's Meow, which struck us as funny. Inside, a furious karaoke battle was under way.

In Italy, I've always hated karaoke, but here I was in seventh heaven. As I leafed through the book of music, I found the Beatles, James Taylor, Dan Fogelberg, the Eagles, Alabama, Jackson Browne . . . As we drank one toast and then another, the place filled up. An audience was shouting with excitement, ready to applaud the performance of aspiring singers.

At some point in the evening, I stepped away to visit the bathroom, and when I came back I was greeted by a situation that might reasonably have caused a nervous breakdown: everyone in the club was looking expectantly in my direction, as the blond emcee had just called my name to come up on the stage and sing! My two bastard friends had put in my name while I, all unsuspecting, was off in the bathroom. They were happily applauding from the safety of the far end of the club. I hovered there, un-decided whether to take to my heels or accept induction into the Hall of Shame.

I opted for the latter—I certainly couldn't disappoint a roomful of screaming fans. The emcee was whipping them into a frenzy, urging them to "give it up for Luca from Rome," while I stood there shaking like a leaf, microphone in hand, waiting to be told what I would be expected to sing. My anguish was short-lived. After a few seconds of a twelve-string guitar riff, soon joined by a wailing electric guitar, I recognized the piece. Overjoyed, I summoned all the voice I could muster and belted out: *"Well, I tried to make it Sunday, but I got so damn depressed, that I set my sights on Monday and I got myself undressed."* It was "Sister Golden Hair" by America, and there, in New Orleans, for a few enchanted minutes, I *was* Gerry Beckley. The audi-ence smiled, clapped, and gave me the thumbs-up while on the monitor the lyrics of the song spooled by—though I had no need for them. Luca Spaghetti was singing "Sister Golden Hair" by America at the Cat's Meow in New Or-leans, and no one seemed to be making a move to toss him out of the place! At least, not yet.

When I finished my rendition to a wave of applause, I was in a state of complete exaltation. I wanted to stay on the stage for the next three days, like at Woodstock. I wanted to serenade New Orleans with one song after an-other, but my own good sense and the angry glares of the other singers on the list suggested it might be time to get the hell off the stage.

I went back to the table and embraced my prankster friends. I thanked them for volunteering my services. They said nothing; they just handed me the tape they had just made of my performance.

That evening, determined to miss nothing, we went to the temple of New Orleans jazz: Preservation Hall. A truly classic venue where patrons could savor authentic traditional jazz, it was run by a group of exceptional musicians who would take any request from the audience, for the donation of a dollar. The band was led by an old woman playing the piano, and they shared some unforgettable musical memories with us. I didn't know the titles of a lot of those songs, but I had heard them dozens of times in my own home on my father's record player. That night at Preservation Hall is still one of our most beautiful memories of that trip, for the music we heard and the magical atmosphere of that historic place.

From New Orleans, still aboard our trusty Greyhound, we continued north to Nashville, the capital of Tennessee and of country music. I forced the guys to tour the Country Music Hall of Fame and the Grand Ole Opry with me. We spent the evening at the Wildhorse Saloon, where we watched a line dance class. Now, if there's one thing I have absolutely no gift for, it's dancing. A broom handle on a dance floor would probably be more graceful than me. Still, I was fascinated by line dancing. It was a group dance, everyone moved in unison—old people and young people together—and, of course, only country music played in the background. Maybe I'd give it a try someday. But not that night. It was too late, and my friends—more because they were sick of country music than genuinely tired—made me say good-bye to Nashville and we set off for our next destination.

As we drove northward, I almost felt as if we were inside the lyrics of John Denver's "Take Me Home, Country Roads": *"Life is old there, older than the trees, younger than the mountains, growin' like a breeze."*

We drove through Washington, D.C., and into Philadelphia, where we would finally meet up with Bernie.

12

≈

Country Road

ernie was an American friend I'd met during his time in Rome a few years earlier; he was spending that summer at home in Philadelphia. Bernie must have been around forty and was our height, about six feet, but instead of weighing 165 pounds he weighed quite a bit more. His physical bulk and his amiable face made him resemble John Goodman.

Bernie was a priest. He spoke seven languages, including American sign language, and was very proud of the fact. We had met him in Rome, at our parish church. At noon every Saturday, playing soccer with our friends on the little field, we could hardly help but notice this odd overgrown lad dressed like a Boy Scout. Only later did we discover he was a priest, and extraordinarily likable.

Equally out of the ordinary were his dreams and ambitions. One of his dreams, for instance, was to become a character on *Star Trek*: the chaplain of the Starship *Enterprise*. Unfortunately, when we met Captain Kirk in New York, we hadn't managed to put in a good word for our friend back in Rome. But Bernie never gave up. Every year he attended the STIC Convention, the meeting of the *Star Trek* Italian Club. All the fans and experts on the *Star Trek* saga show up dressed as their favorite characters. We always knew in advance what Bernie's costume was going to be. Every so often we got a glimpse of his creations. We were always bowled over by the incredible attention to detail he lavished on them. We wondered how his big, clumsy-looking hands could cut, glue, and stitch things the size of a pinhead. It was astonishing.

He also had a deep and abiding love of trains. Real trains and model trains. He knew absolutely everything about trains. He was proud that he had actually driven more than one real train, and we were proud of him after seeing what he was hiding away in the basement of his house in Magnolia, New Jersey, near Philadelphia: a giant model train set the size of the entire basement, with tiny trains chasing each other along yards and yards of winding tracks, whistling feverishly the whole time. It was an entire city built down to the smallest details by his miraculous hands, his patience, using tons of model trains and other various accessories purchased over the years.

Padre Bernie would be glad to give us a place to stay for a couple of days outside of Philadelphia. After showing us around the house in Magnolia, where he had been born and had grown up, he took us out to dinner at a Mexican restaurant. When it came time to order drinks, vaunting our experience with Mexican alcoholic beverages in Tijuana, we suggested he have a delicious frozen margarita, but he ordered a Long Island iced tea, to our general, if still respectful, dismay.

When the waitress brought our drinks, I couldn't keep my opinion to myself. Confident that I was expressing the views of Alessandro and Corrado as well, I said to him, "Bernie, *porca miseria*, how can you eat nachos, burritos, tacos, and fajitas with nothing to drink but a glass of iced tea? Haven't you learned anything from living in Rome?"

After smothering his initial impulse to break out in laughter, Bernie answered, "Well, I'll explain to you how I can do it. You don't seem to be aware that a Long Island iced tea doesn't have any iced tea in it. It's a very strong cocktail, with five varieties of liquor in it, plus a splash of Coca-Cola!"

A few seconds later there emerged, in unison, from all three of our mouths, slack-jawed in astonishment, an exaggerated choral and *romanissimo* "*Mortacci tua!*" of admiration. He had just imparted a very adroit and masterful little lesson. An expert alcoholic to three ignorant, presumptuous, fuzzy-chinned amateurs.

Dinner was very enjoyable. While we were eating, we told Bernie all about the marvelous fast-food place we had discovered in Santa Barbara, and how Signore Hooters had become our new personal hero. Once again, Bernie set us straight. With a cocked eyebrow, he asked us the exact spelling of this remarkable surname. "H-o-o-t-e-r-s," I spelled it out for him. Bernie burst into helpless laughter, and after he finally caught his breath, the three of us finally understood what dummies we had been!

A Roman Catholic priest had just patiently explained to us what *tits* were known as in American English slang.

We toured Philadelphia—"Philly" to its friends—the following day, and we really liked the city. We covered miles and miles on foot, and it wasn't until that night, after dinner, that Bernie played the ace he had kept up his sleeve for this very moment. We found ourselves standing outside a warehouse. Frantic, fast-beat music could be heard inside. But it wasn't until we opened the doors to go in that I realized to what earthly paradise my friend the priest had brought us: it was a line dancing club! Inside there were hundreds of people wearing cowboy boots and ten-gallon hats, clustered around a sort of ring, where dozens and dozens of smiling people were doing a perfectly synchronized line dance to the notes of "Take It Easy."

For the first time in my life, I felt like dancing, but there was just no way. It was too challenging. However simple the group movements might appear at first glance, the steps changed as "my" songs followed one after another, and the cowboy dancers always seemed to know exactly where to go and what to do, which foot to turn on, whether to stamp the floor with heel or toe, whether to moved forward in a row or wheel in a circle. It was wonderful! Captivating! Phenomenal! I could feel the spirit of Tony Manero possessing me . . . We stayed there for hours, enjoying this amazing choral spectacle, and once or twice I even managed to tap my foot to the music.

After that fantastic evening, we said good-bye to Padre Bernie and thanked him for his warm hospitality. We invited him back to Rome, and soon.

The time had come for Boston.

I was especially eager for this part of the trip. Ten years earlier I had bought a book with music and lyrics, chords, charts, and a brief biography of some singer-songwriter who happened to have caught my fancy. Can you guess who it was? Here are the opening words of that book: "James Taylor was born on March 12, 1948, at 5:06 p.m. at Boston General Hospital." Here was my chance. I was going to go see the birthplace of my personal idol. I know, I know—James Taylor lived for many years in Chapel Hill, North Carolina. But it all began right here, in Boston, Massachusetts.

Of course, I had prepared my two lieutenants to escort me like a king on this mission. Since I'd been unsuccessful in Manhattan, maybe here, in Boston, I would manage to run into James himself, perhaps walking down the street on a quick trip back to his native city, or else on the sidewalk on Martha's Vineyard, *or else on the turnpike from Stockbridge to Boston.* Boston was beautiful, with the ocean stretching out—a young, green, friendly city. We immediately set out to follow the Freedom Trail, a redbrick walking route connecting all the principal historic sites of the city. As we made our way along it, a series of notions about American history surfaced in our memories from school days, first and foremost the Tea Act, which made Boston a fundamental landmark in the history of American independence. But what impressed us in particular was the Faneuil Hall Marketplace, with Quincy Market, where you could find food and delicacies of all kinds. There were historic restaurants serving traditional seafood, including one of my all-time favorite American dishes, clam chowder.

But there was no trace of JT in Boston.

The next day, as we were driving to the Prudential Center to see Boston from high above, I suddenly glimpsed a building I had forgotten all about: Boston General Hospital. I felt as if I'd reached the destination of my pilgrimage—I had found my little grotto of Bethlehem! Seized by an uncontrollable wave of excitement, I forced my two unfortunate friends to get out of the car and tiptoe up to the front entrance with me. They accompanied me with a look on their faces that betrayed a mixture of emotions: an awareness that their patience was coming to an end, and an abiding concern for my state of mental health.

They didn't get it, and there was nothing I could do about that.

And in fact, that afternoon, as soon as we got back in

the car and pulled around the corner, far from prying eyes, my two friends beat me up.

The next morning we started south to our home away from home, New York. First, though, we stopped on Cape Cod, the beautiful peninsula south and east of Boston. The ocean breezes and maritime atmosphere made us think of our old friend Jessica Fletcher, or the "Lady in Yellow," as she's known in Italy. *Murder, She Wrote* was one of our favorite American TV shows, Aunt Jessica solving murders with an irresistible blend of cunning and imperturbable resolve.

Once we got back to Pat's house, we immediately recognized a wonderful smell wafting out of the kitchen—an aroma that had once been so familiar . . . the inimitable essence of tomato sauce! We were finally going to eat pasta again! This time, it was lovingly prepared by the hands of our dear friend Patrick. One day, I'd like to do a study to determine how long an Italian can survive without pasta, especially an Italian named Luca Spaghetti.

Well, here's one data point: if it's Patrick's pasta we're talking about . . . a long, long time! The quantity of pennette that he ladled into our bowls was more than sufficient to feed an army. But as far as cooking pasta sauce is concerned, forget Patrick—give me Patrick's mom. No, my friend was no pasta chef. I actually fell asleep that night dreaming of Amtrak pepperoni pizza.

Un Amico Italiano

What a strange sensation to come back to New York after such an intense month away, so many thrills and new discoveries, so many interesting people and unforgettable places. I felt like I'd left New York a boy and come back a little more of a man. And I was starting to feel a hint of sadness—I was soon going to have to say good-bye to this place I loved so well. Yes, the American dream of this Italian boy was about to come to an end.

A few days later, as the plane taxied into position for takeoff, I reflected on how fast that trip had gone by. I thought of the oceans, the deserts, the bridges, the skyscrapers, the Grand Canyon, Pat, Bernie, Luis, little Steve, the Yankees, the legendary Signore Hooters, "Sister Golden Hair," and Preservation Hall.

The airplane started rolling forward. As it moved down the runway it gradually picked up speed, and for a moment I wished I hadn't just felt the landing gear separating from the cement. I looked out the window and saw the sunset illuminating Manhattan with a reddish light. The island dwindled into the distance, and I closed my eyes. I wanted to trap the two tears I thought were still welling up. In reality, though, they were already running down my cheeks.

13

Hard Times

$\mathcal{C}$oming home was upsetting. I felt like I didn't really belong back home anymore, after gorging myself on America, a delicious monthlong journey I'd never forget. Now it was time for me to decide what to do with the rest of my life—I had a business degree safely tucked away, with the diploma ready to hang on the wall of my office. But which office? In a bank? As an entrepreneur in business for himself? I thought it over for a long, long time, months in which I was trapped between my anguish over the future and my yearning for the United States. In the end, I decided I would go into business for myself. Of course, it wouldn't be easy to build a professional clientele from scratch. In Italy, it's more customary to inherit a busi-ness. But all things considered, that's what I wanted to do: become a tax accountant. That's right, a colorless, jacket-

and-tie-wearing counter of other people's money. But who was likely to entrust their hard-earned cash to someone named Spaghetti? Well, there'd be time to worry about that later. In the meantime, I started my three-year apprenticeship in an accounting firm. The one certainty that this new chapter in my life brought to me was this: the dream was well and truly over.

During that first period of uncertainty, I began abandoning myself to another array of dreams.

With my last name, I reasoned, couldn't I devote myself to a line of work that was a little more imaginative than accounting? I started asking myself, *Luca, does your last name suggest anything to you?* I thought it was far too obvious to open a restaurant in Rome and call it Da Spaghetti; deep in my subconscious, I must have been yearning to break away from the dead weight of my surname, so I was keeping that idea of starting a restaurant safe in my vest pocket, as a last-ditch alternative if nothing else worked out. Still, I kept coming back to it in my mind, this odd dream. I wondered why my father, and his father's father— all of them named Spaghetti—had never thought of starting a restaurant.

I could follow in Signore Hooters's footsteps. I wouldn't have spectacularly pneumatic young waitresses serving hamburgers; instead, I'd open a new fast-food chain in the United States, with restaurants everywhere, in all fifty states, serving nothing but pasta: *Luca Spaghetti's!*

The basic concept would be very simple: a menu with

two columns. In column A, all the varieties of pasta—long, short, fresh, stuffed—and in column B, the various types of sauce—obviously traditional Italian sauces, including carbonara, amatriciana, ragù, pesto, and so on. The happy customers would have the fun of selecting the mix of pasta and sauce best suited to their personal taste buds. There would be all kinds of combos, including the fabulous Spaghetti Combo, a secret combination that I refuse to share with the world.

And my name, on the signs of all the Luca Spaghetti's fast-food outlets, would especially enjoy pride of place on Fifth Avenue, between Bulgari and Tiffany's. For that matter, I challenge anyone to deny that a bowl of spaghetti, cooked properly, is not a priceless jewel.

But life had something very different in store for me. And that was . . . wait for it . . . the Italian *fisco*, Italy's equivalent of the Internal Revenue Service in the United States, an institution I deal with every day of my working life. The Italian tax system, in case you don't know this already, is a nightmare world, a quagmire abounding in laws, regulations, clauses, and subchapters written in a language that is completely incomprehensible gobbledygook for 90 percent of the country's taxpayers. As a result, those taxpayers turn frantically for explanations, clarifications, and reassurance to the one person who has volunteered for this form of secular martyrdom: their tax accountant. In response, the tax accountant thinks long and hard about how best to translate and interpret for his clients the latest generation of fiscal bullshit—and usually gives up in complete frustration.

Then comes the long and intricate process of registering all the documents, the patient interminable calculations involved, the culminating archiving of every piece of paper used in the process. And all that is merely the lead-up to the horrifying period that runs from April to July, when tax accountants become the most hated and feared people in all Italy. That is when we file our tax returns. And this agreeable system has only one purpose: to get the Italian people to pay their taxes. In return, the Italian people like to heap insults and curses on the heads of their unfortunate and completely innocent tax accountants. So every year, around mid-April, I don my tax accountant armor, helmet, and shield, ready to receive my annual ration of insults. It doesn't end until my clients go on their summer vacation. That is, provided they have any money left to go on vacation, once I'm done with them.

I have to confess that when one of my clients is especially obnoxious, it's almost a pleasure to make them pay their taxes. Especially if they're money-grubbers. In those cases, I feel a subtle sadistic enjoyment when it's time to call them in late May, and I can sense them quaking in their shoes on the other end of the line, preparing themselves mentally for the earthshaking number I am about to pronounce.

You can never predict a Roman's reaction to taxes. One of the few things that buck up my courage is a phrase that Albert Einstein himself once uttered: "The hardest thing in the world to understand is the income tax." It's true; Einstein was right. As a tax accountant, I've seen things you wouldn't believe. I've seen taxpayers turn white as a sheet and nearly faint when informed of the amount of tax due, others fall to their knees and supplicate me to "do something"; I've listened to the delirious rantings of people convinced of the existence of phantom laws and fiscal deductions created especially for them, and I've sat in silence with others, stunned and unbelieving at the thought that roughly half their earnings would vanish into thin air.

In a sense, perhaps the best clients are the ones who just don't want to know: the more their tax accountant works to make them aware of deadlines, balance sheets, and tax returns, the worse their headache gets and the louder they shout that they just don't want to hear about it, they trust their accountant implicitly with a blind faith, and they'll pay whatever he says to pay, file the returns he recommends filing without batting an eye the instant he says it's time. But we tax accountants know that while part of that reasoning may be true—the part about not wanting to know—when the time comes to pay, most of those clients will just slip right into another category: the supplicants down on their knees.

With the most distracted, careless, and forgetful ones, I try to be more attentive. I do my best throughout the year to educate them patiently about the best way and times to bring me their documentation. More or less, they all obey in a disciplined manner, even if they keep their brains switched off about the various rationales behind the tax codes. There is just one of them, my friend Francesca, a physical therapist and osteopath, who is consistently and faithfully determined not to learn or remember one single deadline. She is the absolute charismatic leader of the group of my taxpaying clients who Just. Don't. Want. To. Know. They'll pay and forget about it. It's just that, each time, I have to remind them. And so it was, a few years ago, that after reminding and pestering Francesca for months and months, telling her that this year, like last year, and the year before, she would have to pay her taxes on June 16, I wrote her yet another e-mail just three days before the final deadline: "Ciao, Francesca, everything okay? The deadline is upon us and you're my last client. Will you remember to bring me all the documents as soon as possible so we can file your return?"

She wrote back: "File what return?"

My first impulse was to crack my head against my desktop in sheer furious frustration. So I did. Once I regained consciousness, I started to mull over various methods of simply rubbing her out. Maybe I'd wait in my car downstairs from my office, wearing oversized old-fashioned racing goggles, and run her over as soon as I saw her. I briefly considered resigning from the profession.

Actually, though, Francesca gave me a wonderful running joke. When my busiest and most nitpicking clients—always the most boring ones—call me months ahead of time to ask, "Mr. Spaghetti, when can I drop by the office to bring you my documents so we can file the return?," I always reply, in a cheerful voice: "File what return?"

14

~~~

Golden Moments

In those years, there was only one bridge to take me back to that faraway, big-sky, cowboy America I missed so much: music. I tried to spend at least an hour every day alone with my guitar. Every so often, though, instead of playing the guitar for myself, I would play with my brother Fabio. I have always played the acoustic guitar; he belongs to another generation, and is a little bit more of a showman than me. Captivated by Mark Knopfler and Dire Straits' "The Sultans of Swing," Fabio always preferred the electric guitar. Undoubtedly, some songs turned out much better when we played together, both because the sound was richer, fuller, and because we could sing in harmony.

One day it dawned on us that we had put together a repertoire of forty or so songs that we were able to sing halfway decently. Maybe we could perform in some Roman club.

We decided to give it a shot. The problem, as usual, was the name. We certainly couldn't appear onstage as the Spaghetti Brothers or Spaghetti & Spaghetti. At best, a club owner would laugh us out of his office. Luckily, Fabio and I had a couple of friends who were just as crazy about music as we were: Mario and Gianni. Mario was five years older than me, and he loved the Beatles above all others— he wanted to be John, but to his immense good fortune, he had the voice of Paul.

Gianni was my brother's age, and just about as exuberant as Fabio. He was crazy about the blues, so he too played the electric guitar. All four of us played the guitar— some better, some worse, but each with his own personal style. All four of us wanted to play together. So my brother and I decided to form a band with Gianni and Mario. Our repertoire ranged from the classic songs of the Fab Four to songs with more of a mellow West Coast sound. To be honest, nobody was playing this music in Rome at the time, and so our band would be a brand-new thing for everyone.

And so we founded the band. Now we just needed a name. We ruled out from the start anything with the word "spaghetti." We wanted to find a name that was unusual and original, but also representative of the kind of music we were going to play. Gianni, our leader, whose last name was Cavallo, had a brilliant idea: all we had to do was translate his first and last name into English. And so our band became the John Horse Quartet, and we were transformed into four guitar-playing Roman cowboys.

We started rehearsing. Our rehearsal space was in the outlying town of Velletri, where Mario owned a little villa with a basement space where we could make all the noise we wanted without bothering anyone. Soon after we began rehearsing, a new presence began buzzing around us: Simona.

Simona was Mario's wife. She loved music and the Beatles just as much as we did, and every song we sang she couldn't help but sing along to, or beat a tambourine in time, or just jump around to the rhythm of the song. We couldn't really say whether she was our Linda or our Yoko. Sadly, Linda had just died, and Yoko is the woman who has received the greatest number of curses in the history of mankind. So we decided that Simona could become the fifth Beatle, our own Billy Preston. That, of course, required us to overlook the fact that Billy Preston not only played the piano, but was big, tall, and black, while Simona was petite, blond, fair-skinned, and—most important of all—so tiny that her nickname was Pulce, which means "flea" in Italian. Still, her voice did bring an extra something to our all-male chorus, and her feminine presence onstage would bring a hint of grace and beauty that four amateur strummers really lacked.

Our debut performance was looming ever closer. Since we like to *exaggerate* in Rome, we decided to organize a party in a giant hangar. If things went as well as we were hoping, we'd develop a following and could book appearances in legitimate venues. We hadn't counted on word of mouth, though: when the evening came, looking out at the audience from the stage, we realized that, what with family and friends and friends of friends and friends of family and family of friends, there were five hundred people standing there expectantly, waiting for us to play the first note.

Our legs were quaking in fear, but we couldn't wait to start playing. When the emcee announced us, the John Horse Quartet officially began its career as a band, to the applause of some five hundred people. The lights went out, the spotlights turned on and focused on us, we sat down on our five stools, cradled our guitars in our arms, and adjusted our mic stands. And that was when Mario's voice filled the hangar in a sweet, acoustic version of "Can't Buy Me Love." I could feel an inner wave of joy swelling, note after note, chord after chord. I looked down at my friends in the audience, and they looked back and smiled at me, and I smiled back at them. Every so often I turned to look at the other members of the John Horse Quartet, and they were swimming in their own sea of joy, hardly able to believe it was happening. I realized that when music and friendship come together, they can create miracles.

In just a few minutes it would be my turn to sing in front of an audience, for the second time in my life. So I decided to do my best. In front of all those people, and with all my heart, I launched myself into the first verse of that song I loved so dearly: *"Well, I tried to make it Sunday, but I got so damn depressed, that I set my sights on Monday and I got myself undressed."* Once again, I was singing "Sister Golden Hair."

A thunderous wave of applause brought me back to earth and alerted me that the song was over. The rest of the concert was just pure fun, and we enjoyed ourselves as much as the audience did. It was satisfying, too: we'd played good music—magnificent songs that not everyone knew—and so we felt that we were pioneers of a certain kind of music in Rome. Even better, we'd done it with our friends and for our friends. What more could you ask? Well, to do it all over again! Which is exactly what happened. We played lots of concerts in those years—we got better at the songs we were a little shaky on, we added new songs to our repertoire, like "Ventura Highway" by America and, especially, "More Than a Woman" by the Bee Gees. To everyone's surprise, our version of "More Than a Woman" shifted from dance to acoustic, and perhaps it was the song that we arranged and performed better than any other.

We became a beloved and regular attraction for our "fans." Between one beer and the next, they learned to love our songs, and soon, even, to request them. Gianni found an endless series of clubs to play in, and a couple of times we even performed in venues where real bands held real concerts. This went on until 1999, when unfortunately, with increasing professional responsibilities and growing families of our own, we all had less and less time to devote to the Quartet. We played less and less frequently until, like all great bands in history, we decided to give our commitment to the band a little thought—the first step on the road to a full breakup. Happily, unlike most other great rock bands, nobody overdosed on heroin, nobody drank himself to death, nobody was killed in a car crash.

But in 1999 I couldn't stand it anymore. I had never really gotten over my *mal d'America*—my yearning for the States. Playing music had helped me to get by, but it couldn't make me forget. It was time to go back.

Every time I go back to New York, it's like going home for me. In fact, it's like I never left home. It's just incredible how anyone who sets foot in that city feels like they've become the owner of a small piece of something indescribable, something unique and intimate, that they can carry away with them to another part of this world. Something that you'll always come back in search of. Because New York never stops changing, but it remains faithful to itself and to those who love it.

In 2000 I went back alone, and stayed with Bernie. From Rome, he'd moved back to America, to Brooklyn, where he was the parish priest of Our Lady of Refuge church. Like many other parts of Brooklyn, his neighborhood was very different from Manhattan. Instead of glittering skyscrapers, there were massive working-class

Golden Moments

buildings, gray and brown in hue, and around the parish church there stood a number of abandoned factory buildings and small overcrowded apartment buildings. The streets were also frequently the site of gang warfare, often with gunfire. The large Puerto Rican community that lived there extended a warm welcome to me. Since I was a friend of Padre Bernie, everyone in the neighborhood treated me nicely, as if I were their personal guest.

It was February, a sunny New York February. Every morning, I'd have an early breakfast with Bernie, and then, of course, I was ready to head off to my Manhattan, my borough of skyscrapers. But it wasn't so simple.

The elderly female parishioners of Our Lady of Refuge, who had greeted me with kisses and hugs, weren't so eager to let me go. After breakfast, the minute I tried to scamper away toward the nearest subway station, one or another dear old thing was waiting for me at the exit, eager to hustle me inside for the eight thirty Mass. Now, attending Mass every day of the week isn't really my idea of fun. I had come to New York to sightsee, not go to Mass. But it seemed impossible to say no to all those little old ladies. So I resigned myself to spending an extra half hour with Bernie, even if he was at the altar and I was in the last pew in the church.

During one of these Masses, which Bernie celebrated in Spanish, my friend astounded me with something only he could come up with. During the exchange of the sign of peace, I had shaken hands with all my smiling little old parishioners. I still needed to shake hands with my friend the priest. I would never dare to step up onto the altar to hug him and shake hands. But I was sorry to leave without doing something. So I looked up and caught his eye. We locked eyes for a few seconds, and then Bernie slowly raised one arm, his hand flat and open, palm toward me. Still staring at me with a gentle smile, he separated index and middle finger from ring finger and pinky, making the un-mistakable Vulcan salute: *Live long and prosper!* It was the sign of interstellar peace—direct from *Star Trek*, in Vul-can! I smiled back and returned the salute. Mass was over, and I left in peace, but not for Manhattan. Not quite yet.

There was still a human barrier of little old ladies. They all wanted to know when I'd be back for lunch. When I told them I planned to be out touring amid the skyscrap-ers for the rest of the day and probably most of the night, they started a campaign of exhortation: "Too bad, you can't imagine what a special chicken I made for you!"; "Are you sure? Today we're having Padre Bernie's favor-ite dish!"; "Are you really positive you want to miss my famous specialty?"

During that winter trip to New York, with the beautiful, clear cold days and the bone-cutting chill, so different from my first summer journey to New York, I found myself deal-ing with an unfamiliar element: solitude. My *wonderful* solitude. Going to New York alone was proving to be a fascinating adventure. To wander around as I pleased, with or without a destination, to eat and drink when the urge moved me, the impossibility of commenting on anything, unless it was to myself, to be forced to think about what my eyes took in: it all made me lose my sense of time. It enhanced everything I felt in a remarkable way. To revisit places I'd seen long ago with friends made me feel a special closeness to those absent friends. I had hours and hours to spend by myself. I had the possibility and all the time I needed to think about people I loved. As I looked around me, I wondered when I'd be able to come back here with Giuliana. In the meantime, between a hamburger from Big Nick's and three or four rides on the Staten Island ferry, I enjoyed my blessed solitude and the magnificence of a city that, for the first time, was mine and mine alone.

Now I really did have two homes.

I don't think I can count all the times I've returned to New York since then. I've managed to bring Giuliana with me, and each and every time I've gone, I've met new friends: like Sheila, Pat's wife, a woman from Haiti, as tall as me and with a smile as luminous as Julia Roberts's; or Giulio, my old high school buddy who moved to New York, the lucky dog, and married a fantastic young Indian woman, Madhuri. All these people have a special place in my heart. They helped an Italian boy to achieve at least part of his great American dream.

Part Three

AN AMERICAN IN ROME

15

❧

Letter in the Mail

*I*t was the beginning of September 2003, and I had just returned to Italy from the United States. I still felt an aching homesickness for my home away from home, for the time I had spent there with my old friends. And just then I received an e-mail from Patrick—an e-mail that would change my life. It ran more or less like this: "An old college friend of mine is moving to Rome for three months. Take her to the stadium, she might turn out to be a Lazio fan. I gave her your e-mail address; she'll get in touch with you. She's a writer. Her name is Elizabeth Gilbert."

I think I probably sat there staring at the screen slack-jawed for a good five minutes. What good was likely to come of this? Instinct told me: none.

Until then, I'd never had a chance to return the price-less hospitality that Patrick had extended to me every time

I went to see him. This was my first chance to return the favor, albeit indirectly. But it couldn't have come at a worse time. My working season was gearing up, my post-vacation depression was raging with autumn on the way, and as if that weren't enough, Giuliana was going through a very difficult period with her family. And though Giuliana trusted me implicitly and knew my friend Pat, adding an unknown female quantity to the equation didn't seem like the ideal thing. Especially since the young woman wouldn't be staying a couple days in Rome but three full months!

And the idea that this American writer might become a Lazio fan struck me as unlikely. Of course I'd take her to the stadium! Every Lazio supporter who sees an opportunity to add an angel to the heavenly Lazio-cheering host is ready to proselytize. And Pat, a die-hard Yankees fan, understood that. But an American intellectual from New York City, used to Manhattan cocktail parties and book readings—would she really like a Roman soccer stadium? I doubted she'd be thrilled to be dragged off to the bleachers wearing a white and blue cap to shout "*Forza Lazio!*" Frankly, I was skeptical.

But my biggest misgivings were these: I love grilling herds and flocks of savory meat at a time; I love full-bodied wines and rivers of cold beer at my local Roman pub. I didn't think I was ready to sip five o'clock tea with my pinky extended with a woman who was a writer by profession. She was no doubt a vegetarian and a teetotaler, and she'd give me the kind of look that makes someone like me choke on my blood-rare steak and my second or third goblet of red wine.

In other words, it looked as if fate had decided to send me my own personal Jessica Fletcher.

In any case, here was my plan: do nothing until I actually received an e-mail from this woman. Then, if she did get in touch, decide what to do. Take things one problem at a time.

And so, a few days later, when I had plunged body and soul back into the dizzying whirl of Italian tax law and I had almost completely forgotten the matter of the American-writer-coming-to-Rome, I found an e-mail from Elizabeth Gilbert in my inbox. I opened it with some curiosity.

"Hello, our mutual friend Patrick said he told you I'd be getting in touch. Would you like to meet? Thanks, Elizabeth."

Now I had to come up with a new plan. I couldn't refuse to meet her, but I had to find some way of heading off three months of five o'clock teas during which, instead of talking about music, food, and S.S. Lazio, we'd have to wrestle over knotty issues of the different styles of poetry over the last four centuries—abstemiously, and in English.

I summoned every ounce of intelligence I possess, and came up with this diabolically brilliant plan: a late-afternoon appointment in Trastevere, *aperitivo* with a draft beer—just to see how the young woman handled alcohol—

and then dinner in a restaurant serving traditional Roman home cooking. The plan was perfect; it would knock out any and all comers.

In case you aren't aware, traditional Roman cuisine numbers among its typical dishes what we call *frattaglie*—entrails and offal. Until the recent past, peasants and cattle breeders, in order to make the greatest profit from their herds, would sell the choicest cuts of meat and keep for themselves and their families the less "noble" remnants: *frattaglie*. Things have changed, and now in Rome there is a sort of cult of the *frattaglie*—entrails and offal are now proudly considered to be a traditional dish. And you can find yourself paying more for them than for a filet.

So, even if poor Elizabeth survived a beer before dinner, she was very unlikely to walk away from a plate of *rigatoni alla pajata*, a dish of tripe, or a bowl of *coda alla vaccinara* with her dignity intact. Of course, at that point I'd generously offer to pay the check like a proper Roman gentleman, but I could rest assured she'd never call me back for another date.

So I put my brilliant plan into effect: "Ciao Elizabeth, a pleasure to meet you. Would you like to meet for an aperitif and then go somewhere for dinner? Meet at seven p.m. at Piazza Santa Maria in Trastevere, and then we can continue on foot from there. Okay?"

Elizabeth replied immediately: "Perfect. Seven p.m. at Piazza Santa Maria in Trastevere."

I hadn't really posed the problem of how I'd recognize

her. Of course, she might be the only woman in sight at seven p.m. on a Tuesday in September in Piazza Santa Maria in Trastevere. But it was much more likely she'd be just one in the teeming crowd of young people sitting, beer in hand, on the steps of the fountain in the middle of one of the prettiest and most romantic piazzas in all of Rome.

So I started to hunt for a picture of Elizabeth Gilbert on the Web. Pat told me that she'd written a fairly success-ful book, *The Last American Man*, and with that piece of evidence, good online investigator that I am, I trolled for a picture that would allow me to recognize her. The only problem? My name isn't Bond, James Bond. It's Spaghetti, Luca Spaghetti. All I managed to find was a postage stamp–sized black-and-white photo of the author with a bearded man, the subject of her book. The impression I had, from what little I was able to make from the tiny picture, was of an elegant, blond, long-limbed woman. She looked more like a German than an American to me.

As I usually did, I arrived a little early. I parked my scooter on the Viale Trastevere and enjoyed the time I had on my hands to stroll through the back alleys and narrow lanes and enjoy the unique atmosphere of one of the most charming sections of Rome. It's always a pleasure to go stretch your legs in Trastevere, at any time of the day: from morning, when what guides your steps are the aromas of the bakers' oven and the sounds of a vast quarter waking up and busying itself, to evening, when the whole neighborhood fills up with strollers, colorful stands, street artists, and restaurants ready to serve delicacies of every sort. I thought back to when I was twenty and I had a job hanging out little posters with the advance headlines of the next morning's newspapers and periodicals. It was a job I did in the winter, and it involved getting up in the middle of the night. There were fifty newsstands on which I hung posters, for a fee of a thousand lire per newsstand. It took about two hours, and I'd pocket fifty thousand lire, roughly equivalent to fifty dollars. It was grueling work, but it was a quick way to earn money without interfering with my studies.

The distribution company would call me, without warning, at around three a.m.; I always did my best to get to the phone before it rang twice. Otherwise my parents would get out of bed and turn on the lights in alarm. Then I silently got dressed, went downstairs, and kick-started my dark blue Piaggio Sì moped. I zipped past St. Peter's Square and drove all the way to the other side of Rome to pick up the posters. I drove over to the Via Tiburtina and began my route, usually starting out from the Stazione Termini, Rome's main railroad terminal, an area that's not particularly salubrious. I continued along the Via Nazionale until I reached Trastevere; then I went through Monteverde, and then back home.

The spectacle of Rome waking up at five in the morning, just as I drove toward Trastevere, was a beautiful thing. Dawn on a crystal clear winter day in the empty piazzas and lanes was almost intimate in its beauty; while people sweep up the leftover rubbish from the night's celebrations, the fragrant aromas of espresso, cappuccino, and *cornetti* fill the air, mingling with the scent of freshly baked bread and pizza from the bakers' ovens. The city awakens, stretching lazily and grumbling audibly, and starts its working day, clearly hoping that the day will be an easy one and that evening comes soon with its opportunity for rest. It's no accident that a famous Roman proverb runs: *Voja de' lavorà sarteme addosso, ma famme lavorà meno che posso!*— Desire to work, come leap into me, but let me work as little as possible!

I don't know how many people have had an opportunity to see Rome at that time of day, but it's an experience I'd highly recommend to anyone.

In Trastevere I would get something hot to eat after I completed my rounds of the newsstands. Once I was done with my work, it was six a.m. It was still completely dark, and the winter temperature rarely rose above forty degrees. (Back then, everyone rode scooters without helmets, so if I have a few screws loose in my head, it may very well be from the repeated chills I got during those winter drives.) Then I had to get back on my dark blue Piaggio Sì to head back to the university to attend lessons. And wouldn't you know it, the university wasn't far from the Stazione Termini, where I'd started my rounds at four in the morning.

Distracted and seduced once again by the beauty of Rome, that evening I hardly noticed that my legs had car-

ried me right back around to Piazza Santa Maria in Trastevere. An instant later I was standing in the piazza, facing
the marvelous church and its fountain. But now the piazza was empty, and there was no one by the fountain. Or
rather, I should say, there was only a single elegant young
woman absorbed in reading a book. She was long-limbed
and had blond hair that made her look, indeed, German:
Shit, that's her! I thought. I wasn't ready. I had forgotten that I'd have to spend the entire evening speaking
English—though I wasn't sure what I'd be talking *about*—
and I still hadn't even come up with a place to take her. I
decided: *Trastevere will save me!* Since I was still early, I
pretended to be a tourist myself. I went for another stroll
through the surrounding area, hoping that Rome would
enlighten me on the next move.

Still, the fact that the writer was there ahead of time
seemed, if nothing else, like a good beginning.

I finished my stroll, walked back out onto the piazza
from Via di San Francesco a Ripa, and once again found
myself in front of the beautiful church and the fountain in
the middle of the piazza, where Elizabeth was still sitting
reading her book.

I walked toward the fountain. As I got closer, she looked
up, met my eyes, and smiled. I remember reading her lips,
at least the initial *L* of Luca. The time had come to unfurl
my fantastic macaronic English. (Or in my case, maybe I
should say "spaghettic" English . . .) Here goes: "Ciao,
Elizabeth, nice to meet you!"

Letter in the Mail

I was doing great—brilliant, nonchalant, and above all, unpredictable! I don't dare to imagine the gaffes and errors of those first few minutes, but I do remember that I was slowly feeling more at my ease. Come to think of it, why should I ever have felt uncomfortable? She was the foreigner, the outsider, she would be in Rome for three months (why three months? who could say . . .), she'd find her tearooms, she'd locate the libraries and private clubs where she could find other intellectuals, she'd spend her days reading and writing. I was in the city I'd been born and raised in; tomorrow I'd go back to my office, resume my work, my usual life, with Giuliana, with my friends, my family, my music, and my beloved Lazio, here in my city. So what was it that was putting me on edge? The idea that Giuliana might be jealous? No, she knew about my dinner with Elizabeth, and anyway, dinner with an unknown American writer was nothing for her to worry about. My main worry was that I might disappoint Pat; if the writer went back to New York and told him, "Boy, Pat, your friend Luca is an asshole!," it would have been embarrassing for me and for him. I also subconsciously wanted to give my good friend's friend an enjoyable evening out, probably the only time she'd ever spend in my company in the most beautiful city on earth.

We started strolling with no particular destination. Of course, we talked about Pat to start with, and as we continued talking, I could feel that I was finally beginning to relax a little. Elizabeth kept on smiling at me, the same gentle, sweet smile with which she had met my questioning gaze for the first time just a few minutes ago. She spoke with a calm, musical voice. There was an unaffected simplicity to her that won me over. To be honest, she wasn't really fitting in with my prejudices concerning blond, long-limbed American writers. Moreover, Elizabeth didn't seem to care in the slightest about my spaghettic English; quite the contrary, she was studying Italian and seemed to have learned a fair amount. She wasn't shy about showing what she'd learned.

Even though I wasn't sure about where we'd wind up, I suggested, in keeping with my plan, "Elizabeth, would you like to go sit down in a bar in Trastevere? We can have a beer and then go somewhere for dinner."

She replied promptly, with her trusting, spontaneous smile: "Sure, that'd be great!"

I was saved. The danger of five o'clock tea, even if it was already after seven, was banished once and for all— and it was about to be replaced by something much cooler and more familiar: a beer.

A friend of mine operated a pub in the Via della Fonte d'Olio, which runs right into the Piazza Santa Maria in Trastevere. I suggested to Elizabeth that we drop in. As we walked, I explained to Elizabeth why this street is called Via della Fonte d'Olio. Actually, I was inflicting upon her a form of torture that I had endured as a child from my parents. Probably every Roman child of my generation spent many of the Sundays in their childhood on "excursions," as my parents called them, touring the wonders of the city. At that age, I couldn't care less about them. The Colosseum, the Roman Forum, the Palatine Hill, the ancient Appian Way were, to me, just a bunch of old junk someone had put there for who knows what reason. I couldn't understand why they wouldn't just let me go play soccer in the streets of my neighborhood, or sit at home watching *Laurel and Hardy* on TV. Instead, for some reason unclear to me, they had insisted on dragging me from one monument to another, in a steady procession of churches and basilicas. These tours were unfailingly accompanied by my father's didactic voice, thrilled with the opportunity to impose upon me and my brother—both of us wearing the most put-upon and bored expressions we could muster—ancient stories, legends, traditions, and anecdotes concerning every square foot of the Eternal City.

Turns out, years later, many of those "excursions" had left their mark, in my heart and in my memory. And so, reaching back into the confused jumble of recollections, mixing in a notion or two I had gleaned—and not yet forgotten—from my high school classes in art history, I did my best to explain to Elizabeth that, on the spot where the church now stands, roughly two thousand years ago (to be precise, in 38 BC) there bubbled up from the soil a pool of some kind of oil. There are Romans who still hope it might prove to have been petroleum. In any case, the oil flowed uninterruptedly for a full day. The event was judged to have been miraculous, and so the basilica of Santa Maria in Trastevere was built on the exact spot where the spring of oil, or *fonte d'olio* (*fons olei* in Latin), had emerged. So it turns out that the sacrifice of a few boyhood Sundays might finally prove useful . . .

When we got to the bar, the warm September sunshine convinced us to take a table outside. I was eagerly anticipating my cold, golden, richly deserved beer, but it was with a certain apprehension that I wondered what she would order. I really didn't know if she was a teetotaler. For all I knew, she was about to instruct the waiter in how she liked her carrot-kiwi juice pressed, pulverized, and centrifuged. She instantly set me at ease by ordering a cold, golden, richly deserved beer.

But as we continued our conversation, increasingly comfortable with one another's company, I had not lost sight of my hidden sadistic plan. Next step: the food test!

Just then, I saw my friend returning to her pub, emerging from a narrow lane, carrying her dinner in one hand: an aluminum pan that was emitting a heavenly fragrance. The scent almost made me fall off my chair: *spezzatino al sugo*—a delicious lamb and tomato stew. Not only would I need to find a restaurant to carry out my plan, but I needed to find a restaurant because *I was starving*! For such an inviting *spezzatino al sugo* I might well be willing to break any number of tax laws. It took me roughly ten seconds to gather all the information I required: my friend told me where she'd purchased her carryout dinner, exactly how far it was and how to get there, and the menu from A to Z. The trattoria was around the corner; it was family run—no, make that *Roman* family run—with a distinctly local menu, and very few tables. Luckily, it was still early, so there was no need to make a reservation. Perfect.

I asked Elizabeth if she wanted to go eat there. I sensed she too might have noticed the remarkable perfume of the tomato lamb stew, and she agreed immediately. We drank off the last of our beers, and I happily treated her—after all, she'd spared me the nightmare of five o'clock tea, at whatever hour of the day. Then we headed off for dinner together.

When we got to the trattoria, I wondered why I'd never noticed it before. It had a glass front door and a large plate-glass window, through which you could see the lone dining room. Inside, a dozen or so tables were crowded together, with red and white checkered paper table coverings. Most of the tables were already occupied by people digging into steaming bowls and dishes of food. Outside, the gray metal roll-down shutters looked as if the place had originally been a garage.

Inside, the sound level was typical of a Roman-family-run trattoria. Over the loud conversations of the customers, fueled by the house wine, you could hear the voice of the matron of the house, loudly proclaiming the dishes of the day. I stood there speechless: only divine providence could have brought me to a place like this!

We walked in and took our seats at the little table; the owner immediately brought us a basket of bread and a liter of the house red. I asked him for a menu, and I'll never forget the look of complicit understanding he gave me when he heard Elizabeth speaking English. The leer that spread across his face meant, roughly: *Ah, I see what you're up to! I'll take care of things, and you see if this little American girl doesn't have an enjoyable evening tonight!* He stopped just short of a broad, lubricious wink. I felt like answering him in the same thick Roman dialect he'd wordlessly addressed to me: *"A' bello, nun c'hai capito gnente! Comunque grazie lo stesso!"*—Listen, my friend, you've got it all wrong, but thanks just the same!—but it would have been too complicated to translate for Elizabeth. So I just grinned back at the restaurateur, with an entirely different meaning behind my smile.

The selection wasn't extensive, but it was certainly appetizing. For the *primo*, while he held our ravenous hunger at bay with a tomato *bruschetta*, I suggested Elizabeth choose either a *spaghetti alla carbonara*, *bucatini all'amatriciana*, or *penne all'arrabbiata*. Since the high point of that evening's fare was going to be the entrée, or *secondo*, I thought the *penne all'arrabbiata* might be the most digestible of the pasta dishes. After all, *penne all'arrabbiata* is nothing more than penne—in my opinion, penne should always be ridged, never smooth, so that the sauce clings to them—sautéed in a frying pan in a sauce made of diced tomatoes, olive oil, and garlic, and cooked until it's golden, but never dark, brown, and last of all, with lots and lots of chili peppers. The chili peppers are a crucial ingredient—after all, *arrabbiata* means "angry" or "furious," and it's the chili peppers that give this dish its famous temper. When they serve it, I explained to Elizabeth, you can grate either Parmesan or Romano cheese over it.

Done and done: we both ordered *penne all'arrabbiata*. In a matter of minutes, two bowls piled high with *penne all'arrabbiata* were set before us. Elizabeth grated a healthy layer of cheese over hers; I ate mine plain.

Now, I must confess. The one thing I don't eat is *cacio sui maccheroni*—cheese on macaroni. In Italian this phrase is similar to the American "peas and carrots." Nothing goes together as perfectly as grated cheese and macaroni with a tomato sauce. But I don't like it. I like the various sauces on my various pastas to taste . . . various! Perish the thought that all sauces should taste the same—like *cheese*.

Once we had gobbled down our penne, a wonderful and very inviting layer of sauce remained in our bowls. I couldn't let the waiter carry that delicious treat away, so I suggested to my dinner guest that we do something that some etiquette mavens might look down upon, but which is the only reasonable solution in certain situations: the *scarpetta*, or wiping up sauce with a torn-off crust of bread. As I say, some find it rude, but *I* think it's a crime to let a waiter take your plate without wiping it clean of delicious sauce—and eating the bread you use to do it. So, to keep from feeling embarrassed, I decided I'd have to persuade Elizabeth to do the same thing. To my great surprise, she gladly agreed, and began busily wiping up sauce with scraps of bread.

We were more or less halfway through our first meal, and thanks to the warm September evening, but especially to the furious temper of the penne, the house wine, and the fact that Elizabeth was clearly willing to eat anything with gusto, I was finally feeling completely relaxed.

Just then, Rome gave us a gift, one of those vignettes that only this city seems able to produce. A couple of tables away, two middle-aged gentlemen began quarreling, their voices growing ever louder; before long, the quarrel had deteriorated from an animated disagreement to a furious spat. They were both red-cheeked, a clear indication of their drunkenness, and inevitably the whole restaurant turned to stare at them: the tourists frightened and apprehensive, the Romans preparing to savor the spectacle. We all know how readily we *exaggerate* in Rome . . . The two leapt to their feet apparently on the verge of trading punches, heaping the finest insults and opprobrium on each other in the rich Roman tradition, bringing into the discussion mothers and sisters and ancestors and so on, willy-nilly, denigrations by the handful. Poor Elizabeth seemed physically afraid that blood was about to be spilled; I knew they'd never actually let it go that far. The two men were lunging at one another, drawing menacingly close but never actually grazing each other, never touching; they shouted out to those present, for the love of God, to separate them, to do something to stop them before they murdered each other, there and then, in cold blood! But the finale was already scripted: out of nowhere four huge men appeared and restrained the two drunks in their quarrel, calming them down as if they were babies. They poured them each a glass of red, urged them to shake hands and make peace, and then ushered them out of the restaurant into the street. The last we saw, the two were walking away into the night, arm in arm.

Elizabeth was still a little upset. I cheered her up with three words: "*Benvenuta a Roma!*" Welcome to Rome!

It wouldn't be long now until we were ready to eat the real pièce de résistance—the *pezzo forte*—of that meal: the *secondo*. Since this was a family-run trattoria, Elizabeth could never refuse to taste a historic delicacy of the Roman culinary tradition. Among the various treats on the menu, one in particular caught my eye, one of the most delicious dishes on earth: *coda alla vaccinara*.

Coda alla vaccinara is a dish that developed in the Rione Regola, a part of Rome where tanners lived, who were known in Roman dialect as *vaccinari*. Like any traditional recipe, there is no official version. In fact, any Roman will tell you that the only genuine *coda alla vaccinara* is the one his grandmother makes, and that she alone possesses the authentic, top secret, and inimitable recipe for it. Usually, the recipe in question runs a little something like this: brown a chopped beef tail (or tail of veal) in a *soffritto*—or sauté—of garlic, onion, chopped lard, carrot, and celery to flavor it, then add a glass of wine and diced peeled tomatoes. Cook it for an hour or so, add water to cover, and leave cooking on the stove for another three hours; some will swear four hours is better. The important thing is that when it's done, the tail should be very tender.

There are those who claim that the real secret is to use the same amount of celery by weight as beef tail. What I say is that the only way to eat it so you enjoy it is with your hands, and that is absolutely not a secret.

I was already musing about what would happen next: either Elizabeth would courteously ignore my suggestion, or equally courteously she'd push away the steaming bowl of beef tail (no, you couldn't really say this is food for intellectuals or writers . . .). Anyway, the final blow would come when she saw me eating with both hands.

But instead Elizabeth astonished me once again, happily agreeing to sample a bowl of *coda alla vaccinara*, accompanied by a side dish of chicory sautéed with garlic and chili peppers. What made me happiest, though, was that after she devoured this unfamiliar and deeply Roman dish, with an enjoyment that I read in her glance, she immediately put into practice her latest lesson: *scarpetta* with the sauce of *coda alla vaccinara*!

My plan was failing miserably. My new friend was not only *not* a prim, dull writer, and decidedly no vegetarian teetotaler; she was also funny and likable, and she knew how to put you at your ease. Most important—she would eat and drink anything at all! *There must be a solution.* My brain frantically reviewed the most horrible *frattaglie* I could summon up for our next dinner, but it was a thought I quickly put to rest. She didn't deserve it. Quite the opposite: Elizabeth had brilliantly passed the exam with flying colors. There was only thing she deserved: a prize. Time for *limoncello*.

Many American friends have told me that the first time they drank limoncello was a genuine revelation. It certainly was for Elizabeth—although I think you haven't tasted limoncello until you've tried homemade limoncello, which is not as sweet, but with a higher proof and more of a kick. Especially if it's served with ice, homemade limoncello can be a lethal weapon, because the fresh, sweet citrus flavor, apparently so innocent, can cut your legs off at the knees after your second tiny glassful.

I promised Elizabeth I'd arrange for her to try some as soon as possible, but she seemed doubtful: *Homemade limoncello?* All it takes is a few organic lemons, from which you remove the zest—the yellow, obviously not the white, which is bitter. You place the zest to steep in an infusion of 190 proof pure alcohol in a sealed container. As with *coda alla vaccinara*, of course, there is an endless array of recipes for homemade limoncello, each recipe corresponding to another school of thought. Some people add a stick of cinnamon, others claim that the infusion isn't ready for months, while some—and I am one—think that two weeks is quite sufficient. Then you dissolve sugar in a pot of lukewarm water until you obtain simple syrup; let it cool. Mix the simple syrup with the zest infusion, and the nectar is ready.

After we'd drained off our richly deserved lemon-flavored trophy, we both felt like taking a walk—what better setting than Trastevere for a relaxed after-dinner stroll? Then it was time for our next mission: gelato. This time it was Elizabeth who suggested we go get some near where she was staying, at the Gelateria San Crispino, near the Trevi Fountain.

To get there, we hopped on my scooter; I gave Elizabeth my jacket and we set off. I decided to take a slight detour and zoom up to the top of the Gianicolo—the Janiculum, one of my favorite places in Rome. It is a stunning, romantic hill overlooking Trastevere, with expansive views of Rome in all its beauty. As a child, I often came up with my parents to hear the noonday cannon being fired. It was a cannon that shot blanks, and it marked noon so that all the church bells of Rome could be synchronized. Another curious thing about the Gianicolo is that just below it is the Roman prison of Regina Coeli, and it is possible to communicate with the inmates by shouting down from the parapet. Until recently, in fact, the Gianicolo was used as a sort of visiting platform by the prisoners' families.

Since it was around ten o'clock when we got up there, we were spared the cannon fire, and since we had no inmates to whom we wished to shout hello, we just climbed back onto my scooter and headed for the Gelateria San Crispino. We got there in a few minutes, and in what seemed like seconds we were eating our gelato.

Letter in the Mail

It was late, and the house red followed by the limoncello were starting to have their effect, so we decided the time had come to say good night. After all, although I didn't know what writers did in the morning, I would certainly have to resume my everyday battle with the Italian tax authorities and taxpayers at nine a.m. the next day. No one could spare me that.

When I got home, I couldn't help thinking that maybe I'd been just a little unfair. All things considered, Elizabeth was a pretty nice young woman, and I had to admit that we'd had an unexpectedly enjoyable evening together. So, after all, I'd be glad to see her again.

I decided that the next day I'd send her an e-mail to thank her for the walk, the beer, the dinner, the ice cream, and the lovely conversation.

I fell asleep without thinking of the tasks that faced me the next day, which rarely happens to me. In the office the following morning, I checked my e-mail, and I was surprised to find a message from Elizabeth:

"Ciao Luca, thanks so much for the lovely evening, the beer, the dinner, the ice cream, and the wonderful conversation. See you soon. Liz."

Okay, Elizabeth. From now on for me you'll be Liz.

16

⤮

Don't Be Sad 'Cause Your Sun Is Down

*A*utumn was coming to Rome. The days were getting shorter, the temperature was dropping, and the leaves of the plane trees lining the banks of the Tiber were turning golden. Crossing the city's bridges on my scooter was a spectacular experience. Even when I was in a hurry, I could never resist stopping for a few seconds to admire my river, tumbling away toward the Mediterranean Sea, reflecting trees and church steeples as it went.

I was riding across one of those bridges when I remembered how Liz had climbed onto the saddle of my scooter without a hint of fear. I also remembered the natural sense of balance she displayed as she perched prettily on the back of my scooter, even if it was her first time. She leaned into the curves as if weightless; she never threatened my sense of balance with sudden jerky motions. She seemed to have been born on a scooter driven by a native Roman! And to think of all the others who have ridden behind me, often leaving me souvenirs such as scratch marks on my hips or bruises on my shoulders from the terrors they've experienced as I whiz past lines of cars at a stoplight, just inches from their rearview mirrors . . .

For us Romans, getting around town on a scooter is a necessary survival skill and an existential condition. The Eternal City's eternally chaotic traffic, along with its narrow lanes and trolley tracks, has forced us to become accustomed to risking our lives every hundred feet or so, and to drive lawlessly in spite of ourselves.

Just a few days after we first met, I had a chance to put Liz to the test with daytime traffic, much crazier than the nighttime traffic she'd already experienced.

I got an e-mail from her asking me to lunch, and I accepted gladly. In contrast with my university days, when every lunch could be a Christmas banquet, both in terms of length and lavishness, I had learned to master my appetites, at least during the week. You can't eat and drink as much as you'd like and then go back to the office to work your way through intricate tax matters as if you'd eaten a pack of crackers and a glass of water. Trusting that Americans like a light lunch, too, I suggested we grab a quick bite to eat—maybe a pasta and a salad—in the Rione Borgo.

I felt certain she would like this part of town, just next to St. Peter's. I could show her the Passetto di Borgo, the elevated passageway that links the Vatican to Castel

Sant'Angelo. It was built in the fifteenth century so the pope could flee the Vatican and head straight for his fortress in case of attack. We could also find an *osteria* that we liked, out of the many that dot the neighborhood. We'd choose a place on one of three streets there called *borghi*: Borgo Pio, Borgo Angelico, or Borgo Vittorio.

Liz had rented a little apartment near the Via del Corso for the duration of her time in Rome. Having our second meal together in the Rione Borgo meant it would be a matter of minutes to pick her up and drop her back off. Then I could hurry back to the office.

She was waiting for me on the sidewalk in front of her building. Once again, we were both early. The sun illuminated her blond hair and fair skin, and her smile—despite a hint of melancholy—made it clear she was happy to see me again.

It wouldn't take much more than a few minutes on the scooter in lunchtime traffic to evaluate her courage. I started by zipping nerve-rackingly close to other Vespas and mopeds. Then I tried a fake skid on the slick *sampietrino* cobblestones. And I ran a couple of reds after some spectacular weaving through traffic. She didn't turn a hair; she just kept talking and laughing, admiring the beauty of Rome whizzing past on all sides. I couldn't believe it! The times I'd given Giuliana or my mother that treatment—and they were much more accustomed than Liz to Roman traffic and my personal style of driving—you could hear the screams all the way to the beach at Ostia, and I'd gotten more than one hard punch to the back. But Liz . . . didn't seem to notice.

Once again, she had astonished me. At first I thought she was refusing to give me the satisfaction of scaring her. Then I thought she might be reckless enough to think it was fun. In the end, I just hoped she trusted me.

We found an *osteria* in Borgo Vittorio, and I sadly informed Liz that today, because I had a business meeting in the afternoon, I wouldn't be able to indulge as I might have liked, in culinary and enological terms. We sat down at a corner table for two, determined to enjoy a brief, light meal.

Once I had perused the menu, I fell under the spell of the waitress's musical voice as she recited the unlisted dishes of the day—*piatti del giorno*. My hunger pushed me over the edge, and I began to fear I wasn't going to be able to comply with my dietetic resolutions. The more the waitress sang out the names of the various dishes, the more I found her voice strangely sensual and alluring; I was starting to salivate, fantasizing all those delicacies the young woman was describing so lovingly spread out before me on my plate.

I looked over at Liz, hoping deep down that she was unaware of the trove of culinary delights available to us. Unfortunately, the side-by-side English translation on the menu and the close attention she was paying to the waitress's recitation undermined my hopes. So long, light Roman lunch!

Don't Be Sad 'Cause Your Sun Is Down

The antipasto was a tomato and *mozzarella di bufala* salad, known in Italian as a *caprese*, followed by *orecchiette con asparagi e gamberetti*, *orata al forno con patate*, and a small green salad to cleanse our palates. The half liter of ice-cold white wine was soon empty, and replaced with a twin half liter. Two hours later, we were still sitting there, wreathed in smiles, contented and, for the second time, pleasantly overfed. You just can't argue with it: food is one of life's greatest pleasures. On both our faces was clearly written: *Take anything else away, but leave me my food.* Food was art, curiosity, sensual gratification. Food was love. And to my enormous surprise, to put the stopper on our little bacchanal, Liz ordered a glass of the liqueur that had seduced her the first time she tasted it. She could no longer finish a meal without it: limoncello. After pouring us two glasses, the waitress very generously left the entire bottle at the center of our table.

When we climbed back onto my scooter in midafternoon, I was smiling and satisfied like Gregory Peck in *Roman Holiday*, zipping through the streets of Rome with Audrey Hepburn on the back of his Vespa. One crucial difference: I would never have taken Liz to the Bocca della Verità—the ancient Roman "Mouth of Truth"—even if she'd begged me. Not so much to avoid the cluster of tourists always clamoring to challenge the old stone face by placing their hand in its mouth. Really, I have to confess, it's that I am truly and deeply scared of the Bocca della Verità.

I'm no liar, but I'm still not putting my hand in there. Maybe it was the shock I felt as a child when my folks took me to see it the first time and told me that the stone mouth would bite off the hand of any liar foolish enough to challenge it. Maybe it's the long line of tourists pretending their hands have been bitten off. The fact remains: I'm not going near it.

I'm happy to walk into Santa Maria in Cosmedin, the Byzantine-style church that houses the Bocca della Verità. Once I've admired its architecture and said a brief prayer, I wave a cautious hello from a safe distance to the frightening hole in the wall, check to make sure that my hand is still intact, and take my leave.

Sometimes, though, I stay and watch from a distance. I always secretly hope that one day the Bocca della Verità will really come to life and chomp off the hand of some joker pretending he's lost his hand.

Luckily Liz never asked me about it, and I was certainly never going to bring it up. She asked me to drop her off in the Via Giulia. She wanted to walk off lunch and drop by a bookstore in that area.

So I took her to the end of the Via Giulia, confident that after taking her walk and reading the first page of her book, she would drop off into a classic and deeply satisfying *pennichella*—or midday nap—something that for us Romans, lazy and sleep-loving as we are, is not merely a pleasure but a virtual metabolic necessity—especially if you've guzzled and scarfed the kind of lunch that we just had. And

I couldn't see why Liz, who seemed to be turning into a Roman before my eyes, should be an exception to that rule. As for me, the daily *pennichella* was nothing more than a tantalizing mirage, and in fact the afternoon looked grim. Still, I went back to my office happily, contented that, for the second time, Liz and I had spent an extremely agreeable couple of hours together.

I immediately told Giuliana all about our second meal together, in part to prevent any jealousy on her part, but mostly because I was happy to involve her in this new acquaintance, which I still hesitated to call a friendship, but which was clearly moving in that direction.

The following week, I arranged for Liz to come with me to Anzio, where Giuliana lived, to have dinner together. I went by to pick up Liz, this time in my car, and in the late afternoon we left Rome and headed for the beach.

In order to introduce Elizabeth properly to the town we were going to see, I told her that, as an American, she should be familiar with Anzio, because during the Second World War there was a famous Allied landing there. I also told her the sad story of Angelita, the five-year-old who was found in tears on the beach by a platoon of soldiers. She had been orphaned, both her parents killed in the fighting, so the soldiers adopted her and considered her a mascot of the landing forces. A few days later, however, just as the child was beginning to recover from the shock of losing both parents, she was killed by a German grenade. Anzio still remembers Angelita, having erected a statue dedicated to her, depicting a little girl surrounded by seagulls in flight.

I tried to prepare Liz for her meeting with Giuliana. I told her Giuliana was *acqua e sapone*—soap and water, simple and beautiful. I also explained that lately she was pretty upset, because her parents were going through a divorce.

For the first time, I saw the smile vanish from Liz's lips. Perhaps I'd overdone it with the sad stories. But there was something I hadn't known. Liz took a deep breath and told me that she'd just been through a divorce herself. An ugly divorce—as if there's any other kind—that had completely shattered her, sapped her in body and soul, and one of the reasons she was in Rome was her desire to forget. To turn the page and go on with her life. I felt an enormous concern for this courageous young woman; I felt very close to her. In her words, I could sense the same grief that Giuliana was experiencing, in a sense, at second hand, which meant I was experiencing it at third hand. And the straightforward, honest, passionate way in which Liz told me about the pain and exhaustion of that period of her life proved to be an enormous help in dealing with the sad events that were affecting Giuliana and me.

Until that moment, I hadn't spoken a word to another living soul about what was happening to Giuliana and her parents, out of a sense of privacy and respect for my girl-friend and her mother and father. But somehow, talking to Liz about it seemed natural. She had bared her soul to me;

she had spoken with great sincerity about what she'd experienced. By doing that, for the first time, she had cast a light on a situation that had been shrouded in darkness for me. I understood that Giuliana and I weren't alone. I was grateful to Liz for this moment of closeness, of solidarity, and I finally understood that hint of sadness in her smile.

I swore to myself that I would do everything within my power to help Liz to recover the happiness and serenity she had lost. I wouldn't neglect her; I'd do my best to protect her from sadness. Sometimes maybe all she needed was a smile from a friend. No matter what, I'd be there for her. Together the city of Rome and I would send her back home to her family as good as new for Christmas.

We pulled into Anzio after an hour's drive. The time required to get to Anzio had flown by, and it was a deeply moving moment for me to see Giuliana and Liz smiling as they met for the first time. An immediate reciprocal friendship took the place of mere curiosity, and my fear that there would be long, embarrassing silences proved to be so completely unfounded that, half an hour later, I was able to get my first word in edgewise only by feigning a medical crisis brought on by lack of food.

This time, we decided to have a pizza, certain we'd have plenty of other opportunities to sample the excellent seafood available at Anzio. Right now we wanted to have time after dinner to walk around the center of town and the port.

For a moment, in the pizzeria, I was tempted to order

a Roman-style pepperoni pizza, but it seemed a little harsh to subject my American guest to a fiery onslaught of hot red peppers. Perhaps she really was accustomed to Amtrak pizzas—she certainly found nothing to object to in the honest but pedestrian pizza of Anzio. We informed her otherwise and, intrepid foodie that Liz was, one of the first excursions she planned would be to sample the far superior pizza of Naples.

The evening went by in a flash. When the time came to say good night to Giuliana and head back to Rome, her expression told me she'd liked everything about Liz, just as I'd hoped she would.

Liz and I got back in the car and headed back to Rome. While my new friend told me that Giuliana really was "soap and water," like I'd told her, she asked me what my favorite American word was. Every so often Liz would ask questions like that, out of the blue.

I had to think for a few minutes before I came up with mine. It was "surrender." I've always found the sound of that word to be something wonderful. The first time I noticed it was as a child, when I listened to "Surrender to Me," a song by the trio McGuinn, Clark & Hillman. And then I remember stumbling upon it when I watched *The Wizard of Oz* again. It was movie I'd loved as a child, and I noticed it in the scene in which the Wicked Witch of the West skywrites "Surrender Dorothy" over the Emerald City. I loved that word, and I found there was something musical about it. It was fun, a little tongue twister.

At that point, I asked Liz what her favorite Italian word might be. I expected her to answer anything from *scarpetta* to *cibo* (food), from *pasta* to *pizza*, or from *amore* to *musica*, or else *Luca* or even her own name in Italian, *Elisabetta*. I never would have expected her to say what she did: *attraversiamo*.

I didn't know what to say. "Let's cross?" I guess *attraversiamo* sounded good to Liz's ear, but maybe it had another meaning: *Let's turn the page, let's move on to a new phase in our lives.*

But I can't see it. When I hear *attraversiamo*, I just see the pedestrian crosswalks of Rome, where every day thousands of people risk their lives just to get from one side of the street to the other—a distance of a few dozen feet. In fact, when someone says *attraversiamo* to me, my feeling is a slight surge of fear, or at least anxiety. Crossing the street in Rome is something that demands focus, attention, experience, and a certain amount of luck. But maybe I was blowing this thing out of proportion. Maybe I was *exaggerating*. And in fact, I had transformed *attraversiamo* into *esageriamo*.

In the meantime, I had inserted a CD into the car stereo. On it was a selection of the songs that Giuliana and I had listened to during our two trips to America. Of course, I was ready for Liz to make fun of me the minute Travis Tritt started singing "It's a Great Day to Be Alive," the first song on my CD.

But when Travis Tritt's warm voice began singing, I

realized that not only did Liz know the song by heart, she really liked it. I don't know why, but I expected her to like a much more intellectual kind of music. Anyway, that had certainly been a great day to be alive!

With song after song, I discovered that my new friend really loved country music. The time had come to confess my passion for James Taylor, who, to this Italian listener, has always felt a little bit country.

But the musical surprises didn't end there. Halfway back to Rome and halfway through the CD, as we sped through the night, the voice of LeAnn Rimes began belting out "Can't Fight the Moonlight," and when I started singing the chorus Liz burst into laughter.

"Luca, how on earth did you learn that song?"

"Well, I already liked LeAnn Rimes, but I'm especially fond of 'Can't Fight the Moonlight' because it's part of the sound track of *Coyote Ugly*. It's a good movie. You ever see it?"

"Well . . . in a certain sense, I wrote it."

"What do you mean *you wrote it*?!"

"Well, I wrote an article about that bar for *GQ*, and then they made the movie, based on the article."

I was astounded.

"Look, Liz, I don't usually use this kind of language when I'm speaking to women, but I think I'll make an exception in this case. In America you say 'pulling my leg.' But in Rome we say 'pulling my ass' . . . And you're not pulling my ass, are you?"

She couldn't stop laughing.

"No, it's true. It's really a funny coincidence!"

It really was an incredible coincidence. In how many other cars of all those rushing toward Rome that evening would she have been likely to hear, at full volume, the song from a film based on one of her articles, just tossed into a compilation CD by pure chance?

Then came the cherry on top of the cake. I had also included another song on the CD from Don Henley's solo album *Taking You Home.* Just for fun I asked her if a movie had ever been made with this song, or if she happened to know the singer.

"Now you're pulling my ass!" she said. "You think I don't know Don Henley's voice? I love the Eagles!"

Her answer was like a burst of adrenaline in my veins.

"Liz, this is just incredible! What's your favorite Eagles song?"

She didn't pause for an instant: "'Take It to the Limit.'"

I couldn't believe it. My friend Patrick had sent me a writer, but he forgot to tell me she was funny, likable, knew how to put you at your ease, would eat and drink anything at all, but above and beyond everything else, she loved exactly the same music that I did!

I didn't know who or what to thank. I just knew that I had received an unexpected gift from the far side of the world, and that I needed to protect and defend that gift. There was still a hint of melancholy in Liz's eyes. So as we drove, singing "Take It to the Limit" at the top of our lungs, I thought back to the promise I'd made to myself: I'd sworn that I—together with Rome, Roman food, and music—would send her back home to the United States a happy woman.

As happy as I was when I went to sleep that night.

17

⚜

Your Smiling Face

$\mathcal{M}$y friendship with Liz was becoming more interesting and meaningful by the day.

We saw a lot of each other, even though she organized her days meticulously: breakfast, writing, lunch, Italian lessons, dinner, and touring Rome. When my work took me to her neighborhood, I'd text her to see if she was around, and if so we'd meet somewhere, even if it was only to grab a quick bite or an espresso.

It was during one of these quick get-togethers that Liz amazed me yet again. In a shy but determined manner, she asked me if sometime, by any chance, I'd mind taking her . . . to the stadium! Of course, I was honored by the request, and the idea of recruiting a new *American* Lazio fan certainly filled me with pride.

The first opportunity that presented itself was a midweek UEFA Champions League game, and I seized it immediately. I informed my stadium buddies Alessandro and Paolo that we'd have an extra ally and supporter that evening, and I bought us tickets for S.S. Lazio vs. A.C. Sparta Prague.

The evening of the game, I went and picked her up at the Ottaviano subway stop. Ten minutes later we were at the Stadio Olimpico.

There's always a nice sense of excitement at Champions League games. I was thrilled because it was an important game and Liz would have a chance to see it. Once we got to our seats, I introduced her to Alessandro and Paolo. Then I wrapped a Lazio scarf around her neck and we sat down, waiting for the two teams to come out onto the field, to the tune of their respective national anthems.

The stadium was packed, and the colors and choruses of cheers and songs created a very remarkable climate. I could see that Liz was intrigued, and from the corner of my eye I checked to see whether she was comfortable. The referee whistled the start of play. We "historic" fans were pretty relaxed because, in that period, S.S. Lazio was definitely a stronger team than A.C. Sparta Prague. The game began with Lazio on offense, cheered on vigorously by the fans, but as so often happens in soccer, the unexpected occurred. Before twenty minutes of play was up, Prague was ahead by not one but *two* goals. I'd hoped Liz would have a very different baptism as a Lazio soccer fan. I'd been hoping for a splendid victory, a succession of goals for *us*. A celebration. Instead it was turning into a soccer nightmare. I tried to keep my feelings to myself, but Liz could sense the tension, and she wisely decided not to say another word. Then, at halftime, she told me that she was sorry to see Lazio losing, and that she almost felt guilty about it. I tried to act optimistic, and told her that I was confident things would go differently in the second half, though I wasn't really as sure as I claimed.

But that's exactly what did happen. Ten minutes into the second half, we finally scored a goal, and the first roar of excitement from the Stadio Olimpico fans was more a release of anxiety than joy. The roar for the second goal, which meant a tie game, was deafening.

Now we were all much more relaxed. We even dared to hope, timidly, for a victory. Liz felt reassured—this marked the beginning of her game. Now she was ready to enjoy the show, which for her was less about the teams on the field and more about the fans in the bleachers.

For Liz, it all began when the A.C. Sparta Prague coach made his first player substitution.

The entire stadium had been waiting for that moment. Lazio supporters in the bleachers exchanged glances of complicity. It was clear something was about to happen. In the immense silence, the voice on the loudspeaker boomed out loud and clear: "For A.C. Sparta Prague, in substitution for the player Kincl, Gluscevic will now take the field."

The entire stadium, us included, had held its breath until this exact moment. We could all finally empty our lungs and shout—as loud as our vocal cords were capable—those two wonderful words we'd kept in for so long, firing them deafeningly into the cool autumn air: " *'Sti cazzi!!!*"

Liz laughed out loud. She understood that something extraordinary had just happened, and she had clearly perceived that those two short words weren't especially elegant. Now, greatly amused, she demanded an explanation of that choral masterpiece.

I explained to her that " *'Sti cazzi!*" is a distinctly Roman expression meaning, roughly, "Who the hell cares!," though the actual words are "These dicks!" It was a way that die-hard supporters and fans have of intimidating new arrivals on the field, informing them in no uncertain terms that we're not afraid of them. Of course, " *'Sti cazzi!*" works much better during Italian championship games, but believe me, even a non-Italian, hearing it shouted in unison by tens of thousands of fans standing in the bleachers, will get the message.

Finally being able to empty part of the tension that had built up while awaiting the tied score onto the head of the unfortunate Czech replacement player put most of the Lazio fans in a better mood. At that point we all felt free to express ourselves in whatever manner struck us at that moment. And that's where the fun began.

Because in Rome being a soccer fan is a deeply theatrical pursuit, a full-fledged spectacle, and there is no place I know better than the Stadio Olimpico to take it in.

Every Roman soccer fan, once in the stadium, lets himself go to verbal manifestations of all imaginable types and varieties during the thick of play. In reality, they frequently rise to the level of full-fledged monologues, charged with a kind of demented intensity and abounding in vivid vulgarities. Some of them truly are works of genius. Part of the allure of this free-form soccer poetry is that each and every exclamation is subject to the approval of your neighboring fellow fans. If a declaiming fan shouts and peppers his composition sufficiently with curse words and obscenities that are either well known or newly minted, the other fans will display their approval in the form of belly laughs, enthusiastic applause, or—frequently—new monologues in response.

I have to confess that this art is not limited to Lazio fans alone. Our cousins, the Roma fans—distant cousins and, as I should point out, really little more than guests in this city—know what they're doing as well. Well, they're in Rome, after all.

Of course, in the presence of this geyser of linguistic innovation, Liz was fascinated. People say that when you go to a foreign country, often the first thing you learn are the curse words and obscenities. She certainly was not about to miss the opportunity to take notes on that master class in Roman swear words. What's more, she had a sharp ear for language and considerable talent in identifying and extrapolating from the general chorus all the worst exclamations.

Suddenly she had her inseparable notebook in hand.

Of course, I was chosen to guide her through the curriculum of shockingly vulgar expressions. The course began with an explanation of the Italian word *cazzo*—"dick" or "cock"—which in its most literal meaning requires no particularly intricate translation or commentary. But my budding student wanted an explanation of the astonishing frequency of use of that particular word in the stadium setting. I explained that in spoken Italian it is an interjection, and a rather vulgar one, used throughout Italy, but with special intensity and generosity in Rome. Legend has it that many Romans use the word *cazzo* more or less as a comma in the construction of a sentence. Liz began to call it "the C-word." Often the beloved noun is uttered at particular points in a conversation, in order to catch one's breath, to emphasize a point, or to hammer home a concept that might otherwise fail to be made perfectly clear. Liz was delighted with my explanation. It was one more incentive for her to study her Italian. Or Roman.

I explained to her that the one sure way to learn to use swear words properly in Rome is practice, practice, practice. No better place than in Roman traffic, for example. One very important component? Imagination. She made notes on everything I told her. I had no doubt she was ready to graduate to the next level.

In any soccer game, the biggest and juiciest target for the exuberant fans is—and always will be—the referee. My new student, Liz, still had the "music" ringing in her ears that she had learned in Lazio Fandom 101, the first level of our intensive course, so she could hardly miss the insult that one particularly corpulent Lazio fan, a middle-aged gentleman, sent furiously sailing over our heads from ten rows back: "*Testa di cazzo!*" Recipient? The referee, of course.

Testa di cazzo—literally, "dick head"—is a fine masterpiece of linguistic cobbling. It's an obscene epithet that is not only profoundly and intuitively offensive, but also provides the listener with a clear if grotesque image of the unfortunate recipient. I assured Liz that there are no frighteningly deformed mythological creatures matching that description lurking in the back alleys of modern Rome, and then went on to explain that this hot-blooded, highly colorful appellation is reserved for those whom Romans consider to be not only idiots, but also lacking in respect for their fellow man, and—most crucially—who wear their idiocy on their shoulders with an exasperating arrogance that really does suggest that there is something other than a thinking human head with a brain inside sticking out of their shirt collar.

The choral dispute over the referee's various qualities was tossed back and forth from fan to fan, and moved on from the subject of his head to a considered analysis of his origins. Once one Lazio fan after another had pointed out that the referee's no doubt now elderly mother probably still practiced an even older profession, the oldest profession on earth, the referee's wife came in for a fair amount of discussion, with ample speculation on what she was doing right then and there, during the game—why, she was probably engaged in disreputable activities that were then listed in tireless detail . . . I was struggling to explain to Liz how and why the simple term "prostitute" could flower in Roman dialect into so many different forms—at least twenty, some rotund and amusing in their musicality, often expressed in elaborate and lavish paraphrases and variations—while others were blunt and deeply cutting in their crass vulgarity.

A good baker's dozen of these epithets sailed over our heads, and Liz managed to jot down at least ten of them as they went. I wrote down a few of them at her request, to make sure they were immortalized with the correct spelling.

But the finest instance of musicality came with the next benediction—or malediction—perhaps the first true curse that every Italian child learns: "*Vaffanculo!*" A cleaned-up version of its meaning might be "Go take it in the ear."

The debate arose not over the exact translation into English of this courteous invitation, which I imagine has a precise equivalent in almost every language on earth, but rather because Liz asked the strangest question I could ever imagine: "Luca, isn't this curse word really four different curse words?"

What did she mean? I didn't really understand her question. In Rome, there is no finer insult contained in a neat one-word package, no more complete and satisfying way to offend someone than with a straightforward *vaf-*

fanculo, often accompanied by an arm extended to point the way. And where had this doubt arisen, this idea about splitting the fundamental curse word of Rome into four? Obviously from the powerful voice of another refrigerator-sized fan directly behind us, who was adding emphasis to his insult by breaking it into syllables: "*Vaf-fan-cu-lo!*"

Only a writer's ear would be so finely tuned to words that it could pick up such a subtle nuance. It never would have dawned on me that you could tell someone to fuck themselves not with a single, solid *vaffanculo* but with four separate sub-*vaffanculo* particles. But that's exactly how it had been on that occasion.

The stream of insults and unsavory insinuations proffered by the Lazio fans seemed like a bottomless cornucopia, ranging from the most wildly imaginative to the more sober and traditional. What did finally come to an end, though, was the match itself: 2–2. Lazio had tied the score, but I'm positive that that evening to Liz's eyes it was the Lazio-cheering audience of fans who had won. As we walked out of the Stadio Olimpico I thanked my lucky stars that she had been spared the flower in the buttonhole of Roman curse words: *mortacci tua*, often pronounced as if it were a single word, even though it's two distinct words: *Mortaccitua!*

The term is employed most often while driving, when you're stuck in traffic or when someone cuts you off or any of a thousand other occasions occurs, but the stadium offers fertile terrain for its use as well. This expression, which is exclusively a product of Rome's dialectal subculture, when translated into its literal meaning, is a deeply ugly term: it expresses the hope that the deceased ancestors (the *mortacci*) of the person you're addressing, along with their everlasting souls, might burn in hell for eternity. It's an insult with a particularly subtle sting, wouldn't you say? But I should also point out that the expression is so widely used nowadays that people don't even pay attention to the real meaning; in fact, you'll even hear relatives say it to one another and they, necessarily, have the same array of ancestors who have passed over to the afterlife and to their just deserts.

"*A' fratè*, little brother, *mortacci tua!* Did you forget that yesterday was mamma's birthday?"

There's more: over time, this masterpiece of malediction has even turned into a kind of affectionate compliment. You can often hear Roman friends saying something like this:

"Guess what? Maria and I are getting married!"

"*Mortacci tua!* Congratulations, for real!"

In any case, I had luckily been spared that ordeal with Liz. I wasn't sure that my pupil, brilliant and linguistically gifted though she might be, was ready for a full and proper understanding—and more important, the correct use—of *mortacci tua.*

We walked out of the stadium, laughing as we went over the material we'd studied, the linguistic masterpieces that had just been added to Liz's vocabulary. It was really too late to go out to dinner, so I suggested to the group that we introduce our new friend to another exquisitely Roman custom: the late-night piping hot *cornetto*.

It's a common occurrence around midnight, when you've been walking around town for hours with your friends and dinner is just a distant memory, rendered a little fuzzy perhaps by one or two glasses too many—that's when your body needs starch. I personally am not crazy about sweets—I'd never trade a braided mozzarella or a *cacciatorino* salami for a slice of cake; for that matter, I wouldn't trade Amtrak's finest pepperoni pizza for a Popsicle. But a *cornetto* is a *cornetto*. Plain, with cream filling or chocolate filling, *grande* or *mini*, it's always a satisfying treat. Especially after midnight, when the fatally alluring aroma of freshly baked pastries comes wafting down a dark street.

We headed over to a *cornettaro* we knew near St. Peter's, and between after-game commentary on the tied score and gobbling down the delicious piping hot buns we held gingerly in our hands, we were quickly and happily full.

Once again, I was proud of how Liz acquitted herself. Whenever I took her out to eat, she never disappointed. She was just like me: she could eat and eat and never seemed to gain weight. Neither she nor I, as far as we knew, had tapeworms, though my family and friends have often theorized that this might be the reason I was able to eat, overeat, and then have a little more, without ever gaining a pound.

We said good night to Alessandro and Paolo and climbed onto my trusty scooter. When I pulled up in front of Liz's house, I told her, *"Buona notte."*

"Buona notte to you, Luca! Thanks for taking me to the stadium—I'm sorry we didn't win but only tied."

"Aw, don't worry about it. You tie sometimes—it happens. You know what we say in Rome when something's not a problem?"

"No. What do you say?"

" 'Sti cazzi!"

This time there wasn't a hint of sadness in her smile.

18

❧

Little More Time with You

*E*very so often, Liz would vanish. I'd send her an e-mail to say hello and get no answer back. A few days later I'd text her, and she'd text back, one time from Naples, another from Sicily, or Lucca or Venice or Bologna. When she went to Sardinia, though, I knew in advance. I was embarrassed and ashamed to have to say I'd never been there myself. My grandmother is from Sardinia, so it seemed an act of disrespect toward her that I had never visited her birthplace—as much as I'd like to and as fascinating as I find the place. I've seen the Grand Canyon three times. I've spent the night in Wilkes-Barre. I've traveled all over New Jersey. I've crossed America coast to coast a number of times, in all manner of vehicles and means of transportation. But I've never been to the island where my grandmother was born! I should have seized that opportunity to go there with Liz, but work kept me from going.

Every time she came back to town, Liz sent me a text message to let me know. And every time she returned, it made me happy—happier every time. I waited anxiously to hear about her experiences—especially her dining experiences—in the various places she'd visited. For instance, her Sardinian meals, dining on *porceddu* and *cannonau*.

My new friend loved food and was always happy to explore new cuisines. I was starting to worry, though, about what awaited her in the months to come. I'd known for a while about her plan to travel to India, where she planned to live in an ashram, followed by three months in Bali. The idea of the ashram captured my imagination, as did the prospect of India in general: I love Indian food (especially the way my friend Madhuri cooks shrimp). Still, after wading through meal after meal with Liz as my stalwart companion, I wondered how she'd manage to survive in a genuine Indian ashram.

Well, I have to admit that I didn't really know what life was like in an ashram, but I imagined a forced diet of air and vegetables. Liz, cross-legged in perpetual meditation, focused with all her spiritual forces on trying to reject the wicked thoughts that the devil or the demon might send her: *spaghetti alla carbonara* and *bucatini alla amatriciana, saltimbocca alla romana* and *maialino al forno, orata con patate* and *melanzane alla parmigiana.* Knowing her as I did, I understood she'd have to draw on superhuman strength to resist thoughts of this kind.

By now, Liz was able to navigate with remarkable skill through the sea of Roman culinary lore. Still, there was one last exam she'd have to take before receiving the Certification of Roman Quality, before she could be given the key to the city's kitchen: *pajata*.

Pajata is the name in Roman dialect for the small intestine of a milk-fed veal calf, processed by the skilled hands of the butcher-cum-surgeon, who reduces it to sections between four and eight inches in length. Then he ties them with a string. They are then seared with a sauté of chopped herbs and cooked at considerable length with wine and tomato, until a dense and exquisite sauce forms, ready to be spooned onto a steaming dish of rigatoni. Every Roman adores *pajata*. And even more than the *pajata* itself, every Roman loves watching the face of his guest in the awful moment when they realize the uncomfortable truth about what they are eating.

It was as we were digging into two steaming bowls of rigatoni with *pajata* that I expressed to Liz my worries about her nutritional well-being in the ashram.

"Liz, are you sure you're going to be able to survive this experience in India?"

"Don't worry, Luca. I've built up plenty of reserves here in Italy, and I can't imagine restricting my intake of food will really hurt me."

"That makes sense. Still, you love food! And you're

hardly a vegetarian teetotaler—if when you're there all they give you to eat is water and vegetables, then I'm going to be worried about your health."

"Well, to be honest, I have no idea what it'll be like. Of course, a diet of vegetables and water would be a challenge, but I can do it for a while."

"Okay, but just remember, even if they put you on a vegetarian diet, you can always eat *pajata*!"

"But, Luca, isn't *pajata* meat?"

"No, Liz . . . it's shit!"

The interminable seconds of terror that petrify the gaze of the person who receives that illuminating answer are a priceless spectacle.

Still, Liz didn't seem too upset. Truth is, when eating in Italy, she didn't seem very worried about "technical" details. If she liked something—and she liked practically everything—she ate it with gusto. The same thing went for *pajata*.

In the meantime, Liz, to my immense satisfaction, was becoming a full-fledged Lazio fan. She came with us to the stadium a second time, this time in the afternoon with her Swedish friend Sofie for a championship game, and a couple of times to the pub, to watch Lazio away games. This time, the spectacle of Lazio fans, although on a smaller scale and in a slightly more intimate atmosphere, was still pretty colorful. I watched my friend as she sipped her beer and watched the game. It struck me that she felt at home and that her heart was finally at peace. I was happy to see her happy. I liked to think—I hoped—that I was at least in part responsible for it.

By now we could begin to feel the chill of November, even in Rome. Something happened that was all too rare: I felt like celebrating my birthday. It's not that I don't care about my birthday; in fact, it's a sacred day to me. It's just that I don't much like organizing parties, especially for myself, because on my birthday I always seem to be in a trance. And when people give me presents, I stand there like an idiot and break down, a victim of my own swelling emotions.

That year I was up for it, though, partly because this time there was a special coincidence: my birthday was on a Friday and that Thursday was Thanksgiving.

Thanksgiving is an American festivity that has always fascinated me: a holiday during which family warmth and human connections reign untroubled, a holiday of happiness for friends and relatives who see each other only once a year on that special day—and, most important to me, a holiday during which giant turkeys reign!

I absolutely had to seize the opportunity. I had a new American friend—an excellent, enthusiastic eater—who would be in Rome on Thanksgiving, which was almost the same day as my birthday that year. How could I fail to take advantage of this chance to make a wonderful Thanksgiving dinner?

I started courting Liz, begging her to teach me how to

stuff and roast a turkey. I would take a day off work and become her sous-chef, helping her from the beginning to the end of the process of preparing this delicacy that struck me as so exotic.

In the end, although she had serious doubts about how it would turn out, Liz agreed. Her doubts were largely based on the fact that both she and I prefer eating to cooking. She would arrange to find the correct recipes, with a list of all the kinds of food and ingredients that would be difficult to obtain in Italy. We'd do our best to come up with adequate substitutes. Then we'd go shopping for everything we needed, and I'd take care of the rest.

We decided where to have the dinner: at Velletri, in the Castelli Romani, the villa that belonged to my friends Mario and Simona, which was where the John Horse Quartet had held its rehearsals. The guest list would include—aside from the owners of the house and their twin thirteen-year-old girls, Sara and Giulia—Giuliana, Liz, and Paolo, my friend from the Stadio Olimpico, with his girlfriend Sara. Unfortunately, my brother and Alessandro wouldn't be able to come. At the last minute, two of Liz's friends confirmed they'd be joining us: Deborah, a psychologist who lives in Philadelphia and who had come to stay with her for a few days, and Sofie.

At first, Liz did her best to restrain my enthusiasm. She patiently tried to explain to me, as you might a child, what a mammoth organizational enterprise it is to make stuffed turkey for eleven. The turkey would have to be huge, and the cooking times geological, if not actually biblical . . .

Still, I was determined. I swore I'd find a smaller turkey, maybe a newborn turkey, and it would be just a symbolic gesture. Everyone could have just a bite. So the morning of the party, I started my desperate hunt for a turkey. An old friend of mine who was a butcher soon disabused me of all hope, revealing the awful truth: if you want a whole turkey in Rome, you need to order it several years in advance.

But I wasn't ready to give in: this was my first Thanksgiving and I was determined to have my turkey. As I usually do, I insisted on seeing the glass as *completely* full, and I kept trying in various butcher's shops. The answer was always the same. By noon, I had to admit that even if I finally was able to find a turkey, we'd never be able to cook it in time. And I still had to go shopping with Liz for all the rest of the ingredients, and then she'd have to prepare the stuffing, chopping up pounds and pounds of bread—as per the recipe, which she had miraculously obtained from back home in the United States.

I thought to myself that life can really be tough sometimes. So what's the solution? *Surrender?* Never!

And so I said to myself the single most illogical thing I could: "' *Sti cazzi!* I'm buying the turkey anyway!"

And that's just what I did. But not a whole turkey: just four or five pounds of turkey breast. I hurried over to Liz's house, we did the rest of the shopping, and I left her at home ripping bread into small pieces. Then we were finally ready to leave for Velletri, which is at least an hour's drive from Rome. Along the way, in the car with Liz, Deborah, and Sofie, I was upset. The traffic was horrible, I was afraid we'd get there late, and I felt like all I'd organized was a huge mess, instead of a party. Everything kept going exactly the opposite of how I wanted it to go.

When we finally got to Velletri, I was reassured by the human warmth I felt from Giuliana, Mario, Simona, Sara, and Giulia, and their beautiful house in the verdant countryside. And even though I was bewildered by the array of emotions I had experienced that day, I noticed that the guests needed no introductions. They had already made friends and seemed to be at their ease.

So, with everyone's help, we started cooking under Liz's direction and Deborah's supervision. They were the two Americans who possessed the secrets of the stuffing that we were going to fill the turkey with—except we'd never fill anything. All we had was turkey breast; the mixture of dates, sausage, parsley, and other mysterious ingredients would simply be served *alongside* the breast of our poor unsuccessful turkey.

We opened a couple bottles of wine while Operation Tacchino (Italian for "turkey") continued, and we talked about the event that had led to the very first Thanksgiving, the meeting between the Pilgrim Fathers and the Native Americans.

The time had come to taste the stuffing. A few seconds

of suspense and the almost incredulous smiles of Liz and Deborah confirmed to all those present that the stuffing was ready and actually quite good. I felt a little less tense, even though the ultimate test was yet to come: from my privileged position at the head of the table, I would await the reaction of my ravenous fellow diners. I was ready to turn and run if things went badly.

But everyone seemed happily surprised at their first taste of turkey alla Luca Spaghetti. Liz and Deborah told me that it tasted just like a genuine American stuffed turkey, and that was a source of great joy to me. I know, I know—it doesn't take much. But isn't it worth being joyful when Thanksgiving falls right next to your own birthday and you get to spend it with the people you're closest to, with a delicious turkey and a fine bottle of wine—or two, or three, or who's counting?

I was happy, confused, and thrilled—and once again I had seen that it's always a good idea to be an optimist. What would have happened if I hadn't shouted at myself: "'*Sti cazzi!*"?

I thanked all my friends for the love and generosity they'd shown in helping me to achieve my funny wish for my birthday/Thanksgiving dinner. I asked them all to join me in a cheerful toast, and I promised them that the first thing I'd do the following morning was go out and order a turkey for next Thanksgiving.

By this time, everyone at the table was laughing and talking happily. Most important, to my immense relief I saw that I was safe from my greatest fear: that the evening might be one of chilling silence between Americans, Italians, and Swedes who not only didn't know one another, but didn't even all speak the others' languages. Instead, I noticed with pleasure that everyone—including the two twin girls—spoke in their own language with the others, and no one seemed to have any trouble understanding anyone else. To my eyes, there was something miraculous about it all. At that table there were no barriers of age, nationality, or language; I couldn't tell who was a local and who was an American; and as I savored the magic of this tableful of people, I began to feel myself overwhelmed by a wave of emotion.

Just then Deborah stood up and asked for everyone's attention. She urged us to honor one of the oldest customs of this holiday. She asked each of us to take turns saying what we were thankful for. Until that evening, I had never heard Giuliana speak in public, but she went first. Absolute silence fell as she thanked me—*me!*—for standing by her at a difficult time in her life. The intensity with which Giuliana spoke these words seemed contagious. All the others—Sara, Giulia, Deborah—spoke with equal intensity, expressing their own personal thanks.

Everyone sitting around the table was deeply moved, myself more than anyone else. Giuliana was holding my hand tight and Liz was sitting across the table from us, weeping but still extending a smiling embrace to me with her eyes.

In life, sometimes, there are these inexplicable situations, moments that become truly special out of who knows what sort of mysterious alchemy. It is a very rare thing to be so lucky as to realize it and perceive that quality of a moment when it's happening. I had that rare piece of good fortune. That was one of the finest evenings of my life, and I knew it was happening the whole time. I savored that profound happiness, organically, every second of the evening. I was fully aware that a pinch of optimism and self-awareness can turn a turkey breast into a miraculous evening.

After dinner—just like after every dinner at the villa in Velletri—we got out our guitars. After all, 60 percent of the John Horse Quartet was present, and we couldn't think of leaving our sense of joy unexpressed to the world. We played and sang everything we could think of: Neil Young, Jackson Browne, America, the Bee Gees, the Beatles, and—of course—James Taylor. The evening ended with me and Liz singing a duet of "Sweet Baby James." But instead of "sleeping in the canyons," I climbed into my car and, with three women half asleep around me, headed back to Rome. My heart was bursting with joy and dawn was peeking over the horizon.

The two and a half months since Liz first walked into my life had slipped by without my noticing it. The city was dressing itself up for Christmas, and even though I was reluctant to admit it to myself, I knew perfectly well that my friend would soon be leaving.

So I did my best to exploit every opportunity I had to spend time with her, from a quick beer in a pub to another Lazio soccer game to one of our Pantagruelian dinners. Still, the days flew by inexorably, and I felt sadder with every day that passed. Not only was I sad, but in a certain sense I felt cheated: rarely in my life have I met anyone with whom I felt such a strong affinity, with whom there was such a natural and immediate sense of complicity, with whom such a powerful and lasting fondness has sprung up so quickly. Life had given me a wonderful gift, a new friend, and now life was taking her away.

Part of me wanted to beg Liz to stay a little longer, but I couldn't think of interfering with her plans. It would have been selfish. She had a right to spend Christmas with her family, and then leave again, this time for India. Although, with a note of despair, I had to wonder how she'd be able to write me from the ashram. With all the praying and spiritual retreating she'd be doing, was she likely to find her way to an Internet café like the ones she spent so much time in in Rome?

Two days before she left, I took Liz back to Anzio for a last dinner with Giuliana. On the way back from Anzio, before I dropped her off at her apartment, we stopped on a bridge over the Tiber in the darkness of late night. Liz dropped a note in saying good-bye to the city of Rome. The paper slid away on the dark water, breaking the reflection of the stars, which, magically, came back into existence behind it. As I looked around, I silently prayed to my Rome to do something, to reveal itself in all its splendor—lovely, romantic, a little bit bawdy, seductive and tempting as only Rome knows how to be—and persuade Liz to stay for just a few more days. I looked out at Rome, and I watched Liz look out at Rome, and I wished that time could stand still.

But time doesn't stand still. It calls and you have to go.

That evening I realized that my greatest fear, which I'd concealed deep down inside of me, was that I'd never see her again. I was afraid that, for Liz, leaving Rome just meant turning another page in the book of life: the city and its inhabitants had done their duty, they'd restored a little joy to her heart, but now the natural order of things demanded new experiences, new discoveries. For that matter, perhaps Americans, who live in such an immense country, are more accustomed to living far away from those they hold dear, more accustomed to saying good-bye—perhaps more so than we Italians could ever learn to be. And while Liz was preparing for new adventures, I would be remaining behind. Sure, with my beloved Giuliana, my music, my Lazio, my evenings with my friends. But with one fewer friend.

So I made a solemn promise to myself: I would defend with all my strength this gift that fate had brought into my life, and I'd never allow us to forget each other.

When I woke up the next morning, Rome was filled

with magnificent sunlight. It was one of those perfect Roman days I love so much—not a cloud in the sky, sunshine warming your skin, a light breeze making the air sparkle and glint. I decided not to go to work that day, Liz's last day in Rome—not that I would spend it with her; she had every right to spend her last day as she chose, to follow her heart wherever it might lead her, without interference. It was mid-December, and I just wanted to wander around the city on my own and do all those things you usually put off till the last minute—like my Christmas shopping. I was secretly hoping I'd run into her by chance.

That hope remained just that—a vain hope. The only company I had on my walk was my own sense of melancholy. It was such a beautiful day, but there was a *basso continuo* of sadness, the knowledge that my friend was leaving and I might never see her again.

I had the bigger of her suitcases at my house. I had loaded it into my car the night before to save time when I took her to the airport the next day. So, after buying her a couple of gifts during my walk around Rome, I just stuck the presents into her suitcase, along with a letter. I didn't want to make our farewells the following day too formal, too traumatic; I didn't want her to find my surprise gifts and my letter until she was safely home.

The next day came.

As usual, we were both early for our prearranged appointment at a spot along the banks of the Tiber. I had her big suitcase in the trunk of my car, and she was pulling her smaller, wheeled suitcase.

Every yard of road I covered was a second less I had to spend with her, and that morning the highway from Rome to Fiumicino Airport was incredibly clear of traffic—I've never made it to the airport so fast in my life!

Liz was sad, but she was also glad to be going home. And all things considered, as long as I had her near me and I could see she was happy, I felt fine.

At the check-in counter there was a long, twisting line of passengers headed for New York. We waited for Liz's turn, and only then were we forced to say good-bye. We promised over and over again that we'd stay in touch, that we'd see each other again, and we exchanged best wishes for the future. Then our promises and best wishes made way for a long, strong hug, worth many words.

As Liz walked through security and then passport control, I stood watching her from a distance, and then, with a knot in my throat, I decided it was time to head back to town. Once I was in the car driving toward Rome, I felt like listening to "One More Day" by Diamond Rio, just to dedicate that song to Liz, even if she was no longer in the car with me. I wanted to tell her somehow that I wished she could have stayed even just *one more day*, and I felt sure the message would reach her through some telepathic channel or other. So I turned on the car stereo, but as I did, I realized another CD was already in the slot. A familiar chord filled the car and hit me like a punch in the belly, followed a few seconds later by Randy Meisner's high, keening voice on the opening phrases of "Take It to the Limit." Tears filled my eyes and ran down my face. I couldn't see the road.

When "Take It to the Limit" ended, I listened to it all over again, singing at the top of my lungs and with tears still running down my face. I listened to it over and over again in the days the followed, whenever I thought of Liz.

Christmas was almost upon us, and the song "White Flag" by Dido was in frequent rotation on the radio; oddly enough, the chorus ended with the word "surrender." It was practically Christmas Eve before I realized I had never updated Patrick about my friendship with Liz. I had told him about our first meeting, I had told him we'd hit it off, but I'd completely forgotten to let him know about what close friends we'd become, or all the things we had in common.

So I sent him an e-mail thanking him for sending Liz to me. I told him he had given me a true friend, and that I never thought I'd be so sorry to see her leave. I also explained how I was afraid I'd never see her again.

Pat's reply just about made me fall out of my chair: "Luca, are you sure there isn't something more between you and Liz?"

19

~

You've Got a Friend

"*W*hat?!? Pat, have you lost your mind?" That was the first answer that sprang into my head.

But my friend had a point. I was afraid to ask myself the question, but maybe the time had come: *Luca, you haven't fallen in love, have you?*

The answer was the same as my first response to Pat: "No. My friendship with Liz is just that: a lovely friendship. And it's even more special because it was so entirely unexpected. And after all, Pat, you know me. I eat, I drink, I spout nonsense all day long, but deep down I'm just a big, softhearted Italian romantic, and I'm just sorry she's gone. So I just have to thank you one more time for giving me the gift of Liz."

"I'm happy to hear you say that," my friend wrote me back. "Sheila and I would be sorry for Giuliana, but I just have to say that what you wrote sounded like you were head over heels in love."

But now it was clear in my mind: "No, I'm not in love. Or maybe I am—but *it's a different kind of love.*"

It might strike you as almost unseemly to admit that love can take so many different forms. My great love is for Giuliana. But don't parents feel love toward their children? What about a close relationship with a friend? Or what I've always felt about music? Or how about my feelings for the city which has always been my home—Roma, whose name in Latin and Italian, when written backward—*Amor*—happens to mean "love"? These are *different kinds of love,* and it was thanks to Liz and her unaffected simplicity that for the first time I felt free to admit this to myself.

In that sense, I loved her. I've always believed that friendships that begin in childhood have a special kind of deep-rooted quality, and that they are rarely equaled by friendships that begin when you're an adult, however important and significant those may be. But something unique had happened with Liz: she really had made her way into my heart. In just a few months, I had the impression that she'd always been part of my life, just like those very few special childhood friends. In that sense, perhaps Pat was right—there *was* something more, quite simply something deeply beautiful, but different from what I've always felt and will always feel for Giuliana. If you want to call it love, by all means, call it love. *Another kind of love.*

In the months that followed, I lost my fear of losing

Liz once and for all. I began to receive her letters from India, telling me her latest news and stories, and with pictures of her riding an elephant or meditating.

I was overjoyed. Once again, I'd underestimated her. In the age of the Internet she began sending me handwritten letters. And I was experiencing the age-old pleasure of receiving letters and the corresponding anxiety of waiting for them to arrive, though unfortunately I had no return address where I could write her back. So I had to wait for Liz to move on to Bali and regain ownership of her PC before I could respond, to tell her I'd received all her letters and enclosures, and tell her how contented I was to hear she was happy. And let her know how much I missed her.

And I was even happier when she wrote me from Bali to say that she had fallen in love again. She had met Felipe.

When she told me about him, about his natural charm and kindness, I was relieved. I was no longer afraid that my friend would suffer over a man again. In fact, from that day forward, I was one of the biggest fans of their love story.

And from the United States, once she'd returned home, Liz went on writing me. Until one day in February 2005—a day I'll never forget—when a fat envelope arrived in the mail. I opened it and my jaw dropped: "Elizabeth Gilbert—*Eat, Pray, Love*—Advance uncorrected proof—Not for sale."

Oh, my God! These were the proofs of her book! She had mentioned that she was writing the story of her year traveling the world, but now that I was holding the actual result of that writing, the book itself, I could hardly believe my eyes. And the surprises didn't end there. I started reading immediately. There it was, her whole story, in the book. I couldn't put it down, and I came pretty close to fainting when, at a certain point, I read these two words: "Luca Spaghetti." *Cazzo!* It was me! Liz talked about me in her book! *Mamma mia!* And now? What the hell do I do now? *Nothing, you idiot—just keep on reading!*

So I did, and as I read I kept stumbling across the same two words: "Luca Spaghetti." Every time I saw them, I kind of jumped out of my seat, and each time it took me a couple of seconds before my mind creaked to the somewhat obvious realization: *But . . . that's me! Good morning, you moron, glad you finally woke up: that's right, it's you!*

Luca Spaghetti was in a book. I really didn't know which of two possibilities I wished for more fervently: that nobody would buy even a single copy of the book, or that it should turn out to be a runaway bestseller. If it did turn out to be a success, though, it would be the vindication of Spaghetti! My liberation—free at last of this surname that has been my ball and chain. In any case, it was a very strange feeling to read about myself in that book. I didn't know if that was really me; I recognized myself—no question—but it felt strange, as if I were watching myself from outside. As I read the book, I relived my time in Rome with Liz. It was as wonderful as it was strange.

The book was a joy, deeply moving and hilarious at the same time, and in fact it was popular, then successful, and so on in a crescendo of acclaim. It was incredible for me, alongside Liz, to experience the various phases of *Eat, Pray, Love*'s triumph, exulting with Liz and for Liz as she got more and more exciting reports on sales and reviews. You could have popped a bottle of champagne every single day.

But I kept wondering when I'd ever see her again.

It happened in July 2007, when Liz came back to Italy to do publicity for the Italian edition of her book, *Mangia, prega, ama*. She'd be in town for three days, and of course we spent that whole time together. We toured Rome—Liz, me, and Giuliana—just as we had four years earlier, drinking, eating, strolling, and laughing. We walked and walked and suddenly realized we were back in Santa Maria in Trastevere. As we set foot in that piazza where we'd first met, I turned to look at Liz. She looked back at me smiling, in gentle complicity. That was when I realized that Liz was still just Liz, that the enormous, incredible popularity of her book hadn't changed my old friend at all. Most important of all, as long as that piazza existed in Rome, with its fountain, I'd never lose Liz. We swore we'd never let another four years go by without seeing each other, and so far we've kept our promise.

In mid-December of that year, Giuliana and I boarded

a plane for New York, to spend our Christmas holidays with Liz. We were as excited as children. I'd never been in New York at Christmastime, and this time I'd have a very special guide.

We spent the first three days with Liz in Manhattan, where the Christmas atmosphere was just fantastic. The notes of "Let It Snow" echoed through the stores; the snow and the decorations and people carrying armfuls of gifts made it all so romantic. This time, Liz had the home-field advantage: she took us everywhere, to all her favorite restaurants and bars, naturally, before we headed over to her house in New Jersey, where I'd finally meet Felipe. I couldn't wait. Liz had sent me lots of pictures, including a few of their wedding, and I knew I liked Felipe even before I met him. He had a nice face, a protective air, and in particular one characteristic that couldn't help but win me over: he looked a little like James Taylor!

When I walked into the house, I was greeted by Felipe's warm and joyous voice calling out, "Luca Luchissimo!" I instantly understood why Liz had married him.

Not only was Felipe a deeply likable person, he had another important quality: Brazilian though he was, he was the best cook in . . . New Jersey! His *feijoada* was off the charts. We stayed at Liz's house for a couple of days, and we took that opportunity to make limoncello together, so it'd be ready to drink when we came back to New Jersey for New Year's. Because there was another side trip in store: Connecticut, where we'd meet Liz's parents, who were busy running their Christmas tree farm. When we got there, we found it to be a magnificent location, a snow-covered hill where John and Carole, Liz's mamma and papa, had planted hundreds of fir trees to sell to their many loyal customers, who were happy to trek all the way out there to select their own Christmas tree.

There were Christmas trees of all shapes and sizes and varieties. The minute I stepped out of the car, someone put an electric saw into my hands. They'd decided that my job would be to cut down the trees the customers had selected—even though I'd never used a saw of any kind in my life! They explained that before I sawed down a tree, I'd have to make sure I got the ice and snow off the branches; otherwise they might break when the tree fell over. I slowly got better at cutting down Christmas trees, and before long I was having the time of my life.

Giuliana, who loves Christmas more than anything, seemed to be delirious with joy. Carole had given her the tools and materials to make Christmas decorations. Meanwhile Liz and I were wandering over the snow-covered hilltop dressed in the latest Christmas tree farm style: green trousers, a red jacket, and an elf cap on my head. The work wasn't easy: after cutting down the trees, I had to use a special machine to wrap them in plastic netting and then load them onto the car tops of the rapidly growing number of customers. Whenever a new customer drove up, Liz invited them to choose a tree, and once they were ready, all they had to do was shout, "Luca!" Instantly, a handsome young Roman would materialize, ready to cut down the tree. So my name echoed out every two minutes from all over the hilltop, and I had to dash for miles through the snow to keep the customers happy.

By the third day, I was worn out, happy but exhausted. And I couldn't help but think to myself: *Luca, you've studied hard and worked even harder; you're a successful tax accountant with your own office in Rome. What the hell are you doing on a snow-covered hilltop in Connecticut cutting Christmas down trees and wearing an elf cap?*

It was Liz's sweet revenge. After all, I had tricked her into eating *coda alla vaccinara*, *pajata*, and *coratella*, and now it was her turn to have some fun with me.

I had a great time at the Christmas tree farm. Carole was a silent leader. She assigned tasks to everyone with sweet firmness and without ever raising her voice. After spending a few days with her, I decided in fact that she'd probably raised her voice rarely if ever in her life. And John was immensely likable. I saw an article about him hanging on a wall in the house, noting that he'd hiked the entire Appalachian Trail—he was a hiker, like me, who also loved the mountains. Plus he was the Christmas Tree Man. A sort of Connecticut Santa Claus.

To celebrate the end of the tree-selling season, we went out to a local restaurant, where I split with John an order of one of the strangest culinary absurdities—to my Italian mind—I'd ever heard of: buffalo chicken pizza. After the Amtrak pepperoni pizza, I really thought I'd seen it all, but this boggled the imagination: a pizza covered with pieces of chicken and barbecue sauce! Most astonishing of all was that the pizza wasn't really bad.

Once the Christmas tree farm had shut down for the season, we all went south to Philadelphia to spend Christmas Eve and Christmas Day at Liz's sister Catherine's house. They were memorable days, and we spent them mostly gathered around Catherine's groaning dining room table, eating meals that she presented with outstanding elegance and class.

On Christmas Day, Liz decided to inaugurate the gift we'd brought her from Italy: *la grolla*.

La grolla (the name actually derives from the word for Holy Grail) is a wooden goblet with a number of spouts on its side, usually between four and twelve, and it's used to drink *caffè alla valdostana*, a mixture of grappa, coffee, sugar, orange, and cloves. It's a blend calculated to warm the heart and the tummy. Also known as the *coppa dell'amicizia*—goblet of friendship—*la grolla* is passed from hand to hand, from friend to friend, and each person drinks a mouthful of the exquisite boiling hot cocktail from his or her own spout. It was a lovely, intense moment, and a curious novelty for all our friends.

The Christmas holidays flew by. Felipe and Liz went back to New Jersey, while Giuliana and I stayed in Philadelphia for another couple of days. Then we headed north to Boston to have our fill of clam chowder, and then back to New York. When we got back to Liz's house for the

Un Amico Italiano

New Year's Eve party, we found Deborah and Sofie there: four years after our Roman Thanksgiving, we were all together again! Felipe cooked an exquisite dinner, topped off by homemade limoncello. The limoncello was ready to drink after its two-week rest; it was exquisite and violently alcoholic. It was incredible to see the bookshelves in the living room crowded with copies of *Eat, Pray, Love* in every language known to man. Liz had recently been a guest on the *Oprah Winfrey Show*, where she'd shown a picture of us, and that day I'd received messages from all my American friends. The book had been so successful that they'd even decided to make it into a movie, with Julia Roberts playing Liz. The funniest thing of all, which to my ears sounded like a trick of Fate, was that the question Liz seemed to be asked most often was whether I really existed. I couldn't believe it: I thought I'd escaped the tyranny of my surname, and now it turns out that half the people on earth think it's such a funny name that Liz must have invented me!

Two days later, Giuliana and I would be leaving for Rome, but the night before our departure we spent a memorable evening with Felipe and Liz. Like it or not, Felipe and Giuliana were obliged to listen to a couple of hours of musical performances by the Luca/Liz Duo, and the limoncello probably had something to do with the fact that we sang like cats in chorus. Our set was interrupted only when Liz demanded that Giuliana and I sing "Roma, nun fa' la stupida stasera," a song that she fell in love with on the spot. She made me translate all the lyrics for her, word by word. I explained to her that this song is sweeter and more romantic than a love sonnet, that the singer is talking to Rome, saying, *Rome, don't be stupid tonight . . . Help me win her, help me persuade her to say yes . . . Choose your brightest stars, enlist all the crickets you can get to chirp, lend me your most mischievous and charming breezes . . . That's right, because Rome can make you fall in love, with its magnificent starry night skies, the caress of its light evening breezes, its spring nights embellished by the chirping of its crickets . . .*

"Liz," I told her, "this song is a hymn, a love song to Rome and the city's incredible beauty."

It's a wonderful, terribly romantic song. To explain in English what a *friccico de luna* is, or why *er ponentino malandrino* is *venticello stuzzicherello,* or the meaning of *reggere er moccolo,* was a titanic undertaking. But I know that Liz and Felipe caught the magic of the song.

The time had come for me and Giuliana to return home, after one of the nicest holidays we'd ever spent. It was hard to say good-bye to Liz and Felipe, but I was certain we'd see one another again soon. I also knew I would sorely miss my old friend and her husband, that kind man with a sweet face who reminded me just a bit of James Taylor . . .

Speaking of the legendary JT—you didn't think I'd let you off that easy, my friend, did you?—I'll never forget what happened when I tried to bring him and a copy of *Eat,*

Pray, Love together. It was 2009, and James was once again scheduled to play at the Cavea, the open-air arena at the Rome Auditorium, just as he had five years before. It was a blistering hot Sunday in July, and while half the city was away at the beach, I was already in the Cavea, hours before the start of the concert. Luca Spaghetti, James Taylor's single most devoted fan.

As long as security would allow it, I wandered around like any other tourist in the Cavea, and then sat down next to the sound board, hoping I'd be mistaken for a technician and allowed to stay and watch the soundcheck. I employed the classic art of looking up at the walls, an art I'd first learned at school when I used it to avoid being chosen by the teacher, for a test, class work, anything at all.

But this huge refrigerator of a security officer, a slab of beef with a soul patch—I'd been wondering the whole time when he would have me thrown out—suddenly ordered one of his security guards to escort me out.

This time, though, I was armed. And I was armed with a lethal weapon: a copy of *Eat, Pray, Love*, which I had specially customized. I'd printed all the pictures I'd had taken of myself with James over the course of the years, and on the title page I'd written a few words to thank him. If I say so myself, they brought tears to the eye!

If they'd only let me have a minute, I'd give him the book, show him the pictures, and tell him that I was a character in *Eat, Pray, Love*, a book he must have heard about—and I'd reveal that my name was Luca Spaghetti!

How could he ever forget it? *Capito,* James? *Spaghetti! How can you forget that*?! If only they'd give me that opportunity, he might remember me the next time he came to Rome. And my last name would finally have served its rightful purpose.

But it was an ordeal and a challenge. I gave the security guard my best melting, big-eyed, puppy-dog gaze, and I tried to buy time by showing him the photographs and the book.

"I'm begging you, can't you just take a look? This is me and him in the same picture! Just let me get close enough to talk to him for a second when he steps out of the dressing room—just let me give him the book and thank him for making his music. Then, I swear, you'll never see me again!" (That is, not until the next concert . . .)

Nothing doing.

Cazzo! I'm done for! I thought.

At that very instant, as if by miracle, James Taylor in person appeared, walking slowly toward the stage for a soundcheck.

"There he is! Please, please, *please*—he's a hundred feet away, and I'm the only person in the whole arena. Just walk me over. I swear, I'll give him the book, I'll say hello, and I'll leave. If I do anything you don't like, I give you my personal permission to punch me in the nose right in front of James Taylor!"

The guard hesitated for a second, and then spoke quickly. "All right, let's go. Get moving."

I got moving all right. A tenth of a second later, there was nothing but speed lines where I'd been standing and I was at the foot of the stage. In a hopeful, courteous tone of voice I called out:

"James!"

"Yes?"

"Excuse me, I'll just take a minute of your time. This is a small gift for you. I am a character in this book, and my name is Luca Spaghetti. You will see in the book there are also some pictures . . ."

He hadn't read *Eat, Pray, Love*, but he seemed pleasantly surprised, both by the gift and the short dedication I had written inside the book.

"Hey, this is a picture of you and me!"

"Yes, James, it's a picture from five years ago, on these very same steps . . ."

"Thank you, Luca—that's a really nice gift."

Luca! *Cazzo!* James Taylor called me by my name! How sweet it is to hear James Taylor's voice say the word "Luca" . . .

"James, before I go, can we take one more picture together?"

"Sure."

I was so emotional at that moment that I look especially dopey in that photograph. But it wasn't over yet.

As I was shaking hands and saying good-bye to him, James took the pass hanging around his neck on a lanyard and removed it. Then he slowly hung it around my neck.

I looked down. On it was written JAMES TAYLOR & BAND. He said: "Luca, I don't think I'm going to need this pass for the rest of the day. I want you to have it. With this, you're officially in the band."

I came this close to fainting on the spot. Now the security guard who'd escorted me down there was smiling and rooting for me.

I wasn't sure I understood what he'd just said: "I'm speechless. So . . . then . . . you don't mind too much if I sit in a corner and listen to the soundcheck?"

"Luca, you're in the band—you can go wherever you want."

Now my head really was spinning. My first temptation was to go find the soul-patched slab of beef who had tried to toss me out and tell him, in a cleansing, cathartic, and deeply vindictive *romanesco* dialect: "*A' bello,* now I'm in the band and I'm tossing you out!" But that afternoon I felt only benevolence, even toward Signore Soul Patch.

I sat there in the front row, the only fan in the Cavea, and watched and listened to the most wonderful soundcheck in history. After the soundcheck was done, James waved his hand for me to come over. He went to get his vocalist Kate Markowitz, and asked her if she'd ever read the book. She had, so James told her I was Luca Spaghetti—*the* Luca Spaghetti. Kate was very kind and came down off the stage to sit and talk with me for ten minutes or so. She did her best to help me emerge from the state of dizzy concussion into which I was sliding, but

I only got worse with each band member I was introduced to—as if any of them needed to tell me their names.

After signing dozens of autographs for people out front of the Cavea, James called me and delivered the knockout punch: "Luca, come on inside with us."

Every time he called my name, my legs started trembling. I walked in, and this time I was authorized by the pass around my neck.

"We're going to go get dinner with the band members in a little while, and if you want, you can certainly come get something to eat with us."

If I didn't fall flat on my face then and there, I don't think anything will make me faint for the rest of my life. It took me about ten full minutes to realize what was going on around me. But in that ten-minute trance something dawned on me that I hadn't realized: they were working. Some of them were rehearsing, some were signing papers, and some were just anxious and excited about the upcoming concert.

I'd already had so much that day, almost too much all at once. I was afraid I might be intruding, an unwelcome presence, invited because of James's generosity, though most of the rest of the band might be thoroughly sick of me by now. So I called upon what sense of propriety I could summon, and I thanked him sincerely. And then, dizzy with joy, I finally really did go home.

In the hours that remained before the beginning of the concert, I recounted this magical adventure in detail to Giuliana, to my brother, to all my friends who would listen. All I can remember is the vast flood of curse words they released on me for having declined that dinner invitation. I believe there were even some threats of physical harm.

I didn't care. I could still hear James's voice as he called out "Luca" in the voice I'd hear singing a few hours later.

I couldn't help but write Liz immediately, to tell her that, thanks to her and to *Eat, Pray, Love,* a dream had come true for me. And she, genuine friend that she is, was as happy about it as a little girl.

The last—or most recent—surprise that Liz gave me was last summer, in the same summer that, for a few hours anyway, Luca Spaghetti was a member of James Taylor's band.

In mid-August I went on vacation in Provence with Giuliana at the very same time that Julia Roberts's dizzying smile was illuminating Rome at the start of shooting for the film version of *Eat, Pray, Love.*

We came home from our French vacation relaxed and happy, and I was counting the days to when I'd be able to see Liz again. She and Felipe were due to spend a week in Rome at the beginning of September, as guests of the film's production crew.

Of course, I took advantage of every minute she had free for us to spend together. And then, one day, something unforgettable happened.

I was sitting with Liz on the rooftop terrace of her

hotel in the Via Giulia. We were relaxing, looking out over the rooftops of Rome, and I was thinking back over everything that had happened since we'd first met. My mind ran over all the time I had spent with her: our first meeting in Trastevere, the dinners and lunches viewed through a mist of limoncello, the unorthodox Italian lessons, the Stadio Olimpico, the churches, the streets and lanes and alleys we'd walked together in search of the most interesting places in Rome, and then Anzio, Thanksgiving dinner with turkey alla Luca Spaghetti, the tears I shed at her departure, her book, New York, and the Christmas tree farm.

I thought to myself just how generous life had been when it gave me the gift of this friendship, and I was about to whisper in her ear: "Liz, *you've got a friend*."

But just then, she looked me in the eye and with a fond but slightly mischievous gaze, she asked: "Luca, would you like to go to the movie set and meet Julia Roberts?"

Smiling, I wrapped her in a bear hug. "Okay, Lizzy, *esageriamo!*"

Glossary of Italian/Roman Dishes

Ammazzacaffè—Literally, "coffee killer." A liqueur enjoyed at the end of the meal, after espresso.

Bucatini all'amatriciana—Thick, hollow, long pasta with a sauce of *guanciale*, Pecorino cheese, and tomato, native to the Lazio region.

Caffè alla valdostana—A mixture of grappa, coffee, sugar, orange, and cloves, from the alpine Val d'Aosta region in northwestern Italy. Often drunk in the *grolla* or *coppa dell'amicizia*.

Cannonau—A Sardinian red wine made from the Grenache grape varietal, known by this name on the island of Sardinia.

Caprese—The traditional appetizer of sliced tomatoes, *mozzarella di bufala*, and basil.

Coda alla vaccinara—A Roman tomato-based stew made of beef or veal tail and vegetables.

Glossary of Italian/Roman Dishes

Coratella (Coratella d'agnello con carciofi)—Lamb innards with artichokes.

Cornetto—Crescent-shaped bread pastry. The Italian version of a croissant.

Fettuccine al ragù—Long, flat pasta with meat sauce.

Fettuccine alla papalina—Long, flat pasta with a more refined interpretation of a *Carbonara* sauce. Supposedly made at the request of Pope Pius XII, hence its name.

Frattaglie—Entrails and offal.

Gnocchi alla Romana—Unlike traditional potato dumpling-shaped gnocchi, these are more like disks, made with milk and semolina.

Grattachecche—Grated ice and fruit juices.

Il ragù della domenica—Literally, "Sunday meat sauce."

Involtino—Roulade, usually meat.

Limoncello—Lemon liqueur, mainly from southern Italy, usually served as an after-dinner digestif.

Maialino al forno—Oven-roasted suckling pig.

Melanzane alla parmigiana—Fried slices of eggplant baked with tomato and cheese. Actually not a dish from Parma, but from southern Italy, possibly named for its use of Parmigiano-Reggiano cheese.

Orata al forno con patate—Mediterranean sea bream, oven-roasted with potatoes.

Orecchiette con asparagi e gamberetti—Literally, "little ears." Small, rough, dome-shaped pasta disks with asparagus and shrimp. This pasta shape originates in the Puglia region in the south.

Glossary of Italian/Roman Dishes

Orecchiette alle cime di rapa—"Little ear" pasta with rapini (or broccoli rabe).

Pajata—Small intestine of a milk-fed calf, seared and stewed in wine and tomato, traditionally served in Rome with rigatoni.

Pasta con le sarde—Pasta with sardines. Traditional Sicilian dish.

Pasta e fagioli—Small pasta and beans, usually in a soup or stew. Found in all regions with local variations.

Pastarelle—Pastries.

Penne all'arrabbiata—Literally, "furious" penne, with hot red pepper and tomato sauce.

Pici—Thick, hand-rolled long pasta, originating in Tuscany.

Pizzoccheri—Short, flat ribbons of pasta, originating in the Valtellina valley of Lombardy, near Switzerland.

Porceddu—Sardinian roast suckling pig.

Saltimbocca alla romana—Literally, "jumps in the mouth." A typically Roman dish of breaded and fried veal and prosciutto, with a sage and white wine sauce.

Spaghetti al cacio e pepe—Classic Roman spaghetti dish with Pecorino Romano cheese and coarsely ground black pepper.

Spaghetti all'aglio olio e peperoncino—Spaghetti with garlic, oil, and red pepper.

Spaghetti all'amatriciana—Spaghetti with a sauce of *guanciale*, Pecorino cheese, and tomato, native to the Lazio region.

Spaghetti alla carbonara—Literally, "coal miner's wife spaghetti." Made with eggs, Pecorino Romano, cured pork, and black pepper. Another Roman favorite.

Spaghetti alla gricia—Spaghetti with crispy cured pork (usually *guanciale*) and Pecorino Romano.

Spaghetti alla norma—Spaghetti with a sauce of tomatoes, eggplant, ricotta salata, and fresh basil. A classic Sicilian pasta sauce.

Spaghetti con la bottarga—Spaghetti with dried, cured fish roe. A traditionally Sardinian dish.

Spezzatino al sugo—Lamb (or veal) and tomato stew.

Strozzapreti—Literally, "priest stranglers." Hand-rolled pasta strips, twisted and cut into smaller pieces.

Trofie al pesto—Thin, rounded strips of hand-rolled pasta, served with the famous basil sauce. The pasta and the sauce both originate in the Liguria region.